The Unauthorized Guide To

The Simpsons™ Collectibles

A Handbook and Price Guide

by Robert W. Getz

D1615459

Schiffer Publishing Ltd

4880 Lower Valley Rd. Atglen, PA 19310 USA

Desperately, for Sheva

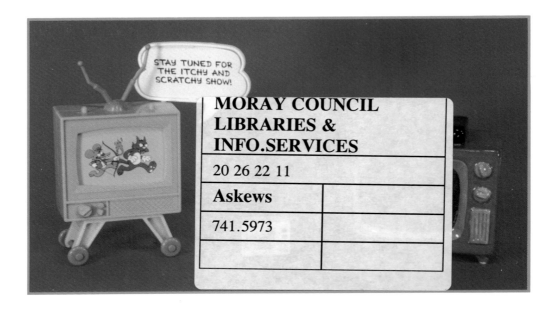

Copyright © 1998 by Robert W. Getz
Library of Congress Catalog Card Number: 98-84188

Designed by Bonnie M. Hensley
Layout by Randy L. Hensley
Quill Script/Souvenir LT BT

ISBN: 0-7643-0545-X
Printed in China
1 2 3 4

Published by Schiffer Publishing Ltd.
4880 Lower Valley Road
Atglen, PA 19310
Phone: (610) 593-1777; Fax: (610) 593-2002
E-mail: Schifferbk@aol.com

In Europe, Schiffer books are distributed by Bushwood Books
6 Marksbury Avenue Kew Gardens
Surrey TW9 4JF England
Phone: 44 (0) 181 392-8585; Fax: 44 (0) 181 392-9876
E-mail: Bushwd@aol.com

Please write for a free catalog.
This book may be purchased from the publisher.
Please include $3.95 for shipping. Please try your bookstore first.
We are interested in hearing from authors with book ideas on related subjects.

Contents

Acknowledgments

Hi-diddley-ho there and many thanks to the following people:

To my mother and father; To Steve Goldberg, who would have cared more than anyone, as usual: it's recess everywhere but in our hearts; To Bob Delvishio, for his hard work and support in preparing the book during its early stages. Mmmmmm, Simpsony!; To Douglas Baptie, for his enthusiasm and encouragement over the years; To everyone at Joys and Toys in Hatboro, Pennsylvania, and the 5 And Dime in Lambertville, New Jersey: now my house looks like your stores; To Steve Ginsberg and all at Claude's Comics; To Victor J. Medcalf for providing many of the items from the U.K., James Koval for games and toys from Germany and all at Lulu Berlu for the kitchenware from France. Merci beaucoup, mec!; To all of the Simpsons fans and collectors who provided help, among them: Craig Vinton, Chris Faulkner, Trina Kubeck, Mike Nagle, Keith Galle, Carl Clauss, and Bill LaRue; To Michael, Danny, Lena and Alyssa, who have gracefully accepted the fact that not all of Uncle Robert's toys can be played with; To George Bond, for valued friendship; To Zelda Golkow, in memoriam; And to David Murray, Michael Nyman, Ute Lemper, Henry Threadgill, and the Jon Spencer Blues Explosion for all of the inspiration.

A very special thank you to Rebecca Greason and John Hein, who so generously opened their home to us and The Simpsons and allowed us to overrun it with hundreds of items both yellow and spiky. Rebecca took all of the photographs you see here and spent many long hours getting them to look as good as they do, often in circumstances that were less than ideal. Without her endless patience and talent, this book, quite simply, would still be a daydream. Thank you, Rebecca and thank you, John, for making us feel at home and guiding us through the Land of Chocolate.

Finally, to Sheva Golkow, who makes me laugh more than *The Simpsons* and who forgives me more than Marge. Your steadfast faith and belief is something I can never adequately repay. May I someday be worthy of it. You are always at the end of my words and the beginning of my heart. This is for you.

Introduction: They Came From Springfield

My goal from the very beginning has been to not get mired in this kind of sour, 'ain't life horrible' kind of humor that is the hip stance these days. I think we're able to get away with some fairly dark comments about our culture by leavening it with lightness. The fact is, the show is a celebration—that's been my main goal from the very beginning.

-Matt Groening

The Fox Network has sunk to a new low.

-Lisa Simpson

Perhaps it's best to be honest from the very beginning:

If *The Simpsons* only consisted of its wonderfully manic opening theme, it would still be my favorite television program. In an age when most shows' openings and closings are increasingly sacrificed for the sake of commercials and teasers for the evening news, *The Simpsons* brings an entire orchestra onstage and goads the musicians into a barely controlled hysteria. It's the aural equivalent of a runaway roller coaster, a comedic express train that dares you to catch your breath. It's a theme whose ambition thumbs its nose at the downsizing of risk that has characterized the late 20th century. Rattling around some mutant grey area between the *Jetsons Theme* and *Le Sacre Du Printemps*, it scorches everything it touches, clearing away the underbrush of sitcoms past and opening up new worlds of possibility.[1]

Okay. Now we're on the same page.

Never underestimate the importance of the music. A theme is a sort of implied promise that what's about to follow will live up to its introduction. It sets a tone and tries to convey an emotional sense of the subject. If a theme's too good, it can make the main attraction seem pale in comparison. For instance, to take a recent example from the movies, Quentin Tarantino has said that most of his film *Pulp Fiction* can be seen as an attempt to live up to the gauntlet thrown down by Dick Dale's *Misirlou* as it plays over the opening credits. If what came after it was not as dramatic and reckless as the

The Simpsons ponder their next move. Chessmen from the 3-D Chess Set.

music splashing onto the soundtrack, the audience would have felt cheated.

The *Simpsons* theme, thank goodness, keeps its promise. What follows it is a pyrotechnic display of jokes, parodies and social satire that moves so fast it almost qualifies as hypertext. It's turned out to be the perfect entertainment for the '90s, a kind of animated websurfing. Just to take an example at random, in an episode entitled *Duffless*, a *Clockwork Orange* homage featuring Bart and two strategically placed cupcakes is quickly followed by a song parody, "It Was A Very Good Beer," sung by Homer, itself followed less than 30 seconds later by Bart doing an impression of the villainous Blofeld from the James Bond pictures. Such an endless stream of jokes about pop culture runs the risk of becoming numbing. Instead, it has the opposite effect, heaping giddiness upon giddiness until the viewer is helpless.

Now, if all this sounds like I've been spending a little too much time at Moe's, stop to consider the following: In a recent ranking of "The 50 Funniest People Alive" published in *Entertainment Weekly* (April 18, 1997), Homer Simpson came in at #10.

That's right. # 10. Think about that for a moment and, as you do, keep in mind that Homer doesn't really, uh, exist.

Praised as the "Sisyphus Of Springfield," Homer beat out George Carlin, Bill Cosby, Monty Python, Woody Allen, and Mel Brooks. A mere two weeks before, in the same magazine, critic Ken Tucker called *The Simpsons* "one of the sharpest, most purely pleasurable television series ever." A month later *The Simpsons* received one of broadcasting's highest accolades as it accepted a Peabody Award. As I write these words, the success of shows like *King Of The Hill* and other animated programs have magazine covers busy proclaiming the arrival of a new wave of animated shows that adults can enjoy as well as children, a wave that is being properly credited to the groundbreaking work that was done on *The Simpsons*. Having surpassed *The Flintstones'* record to become television's longest-running prime-time animated show, *The Simpsons* celebrated its 10th anniversary in 1997 with a plethora of new products, including the

Large Bart, Lisa, and Maggie rag dolls from Dan Dee.

long-awaited release of original episodes on tape and laserdisc.

Clearly, this isn't just another cartoon show with homicidal housepets (well, it is, but more about that later), but an important and influential part of American culture. But what accounts for its immense appeal? Creator Matt Groening told *The Comics Journal* that the show's message is a simple one: "In general there's a skeptical look at people in positions of authority, and there's an underlying message that maybe the people who are telling you what to do don't always have your best interests in mind. That includes people who are trying to sell you stuff, people who are giving you your paycheck, and people who are teaching you the values they hold dear."[2] It's a world view that *The Simpsons* owes to *Life In Hell*, the cranky and hilarious strip that Groening began drawing for the *L.A. Reader* in 1980 and which made its way into weekly newspapers all across the country. Featuring a core cast of a neurotic rabbit named Binky, his girlfriend Sheba, his anti-social son Bongo, and a passive-aggressive, fez-wearing couple named Akbar and Jeff (whose shirts all seemed to come out of Charlie Brown's closet), Groening skewered modern mating habits, office boredom, childhood anxieties, right-wing politics and sensitive artists, all with equal gusto.

Simpson, Eh?

It was television producer James L. Brooks (*Taxi, The Mary Tyler Moore Show*) who approached Groening with the idea of creating short animated segments for the Fox Network's *Tracey Ullman Show*. Rather than use the established characters from *Life In Hell*, however, Groening devised a canny compromise. By creating a human family that resembled his misanthropic rabbits and naming them after members of his family (with the exception of Bart, whose name is an anagram for *brat* and who stands in for Groening), The Simpsons were born.[3] America met them for the first time on April 19, 1987, in a segment that could have come out of *Life In Hell*: it showed Homer and Marge putting their children to bed with familiar rhymes about bedbugs and breaking boughs which, predictably, scares the three of them out of their wits. These short sketches provided a clever and

entertaining way to take the *Ullman* show to and from the commercial break. Utilizing the vocal talents of that show's regular cast, which included Dan Castellaneta and Julie Kavner, the *Simpsons* segments featured a rather different family than the one that eventually emerged. Homer sounds much more like Walter Matthau at this stage (a trait that wouldn't disappear completely until some time after *The Simpsons* became a regular series) and Bart and Lisa aren't quite the polar opposites they would eventually become.

The entire style of these early segments was much more "cartoony" than the look that eventually developed. The faces of the characters had a tendency to bounce and stretch, a far cry from the yellow Kabuki masks we know and love today.[4] The less exaggerated the look of the *The Simpsons* became, however, the funnier it seemed to be. What's funnier than a prolonged take of Homer's uncomprehending mug attempting to process some information? *The Simpsons* disproved the theory that animation had to be broad and splashy to work. Instead of jumping up and down and waving its hands in front of the audience's face, the jokes worked in a more

Inside box from the German version of the "Don't Have A Cow" dice game.

understated fashion. A more subdued visual made the surreal dialogue stand out even more and, together with the show's quick-cutting style, the show eventually developed a comic rhythm that was completely unique to television.

But we're getting ahead of ourselves.

The *Ullman* segments proved popular enough for Fox to consider spinning the Simpson family off into their own half-hour program, something that hadn't been done since the heyday of *The Flintstones* and *The Jetsons*. Preceded by the airing of *The Simpsons Christmas Special* in December of 1989, *The Simpsons* officially debuted on Fox on January 14, 1990, with an episode entitled "Bart The Genius." It's doubtful that anyone had any idea what would happen next.

Simply put, it was the dawn of Bartmania. Kids went nuts for the spiky-haired delinquent with the bad attitude and poor grade point average and soon his glassy-eyed stare could be seen on everything from T-shirts and posters to bumper stickers and buttons. Celebrities clamored to appear on the show and Bart could be seen glaring out from the covers of national magazines. Proudly proclaiming his status as an "Underachiever," Bart Simpson ruled the early 1990s.[5] This is really where this book's story begins.

Aprés Marge, Le Deluge

As the pictures that follow will testify, The Simpsons were merchandised with, uh, great enthusiasm. To attempt to list everything that has been decorated with the yellow, bug-eyed Simpson visage is to travel through a cross-section of popular culture: stuffed dolls, action figures, trading cards, buttons, books, comic books, CDs (and CD-ROMs!), animation cels, snack foods, shampoos, collector's plates, board games, chess sets, production drawings, telephones, watches, coin banks, video games, snowglobes, greeting cards, and T-shirts. The show's continuing popularity has resulted in a steady stream of unique collectibles being produced both here and around the world.

In some cases, especially early on, some of the licensed products were no different than any of the other thousands of items developed to tie-in to something popular (T-shirts, bumper stickers, etc.). But The Simpsons had a better batting average than most, mainly due to Groening and Co. spending a little extra time designing and criticizing proposed products so that the end result would be something that fans of the show would find worthwhile. As time has gone on, the number of collectibles produced has gone down but their quality has steadily increased.[6]

The initial wave of Simpsons collectibles eventually disappeared as people, burnt out on the Radical Dude, went on to collect Mighty Dolphin Forest Rangers and other totems of preadolescence. Perhaps if The Simpsons had not been as consistently as good as it was, you'd just be reading another book about salt and pepper shakers. But the show hit its stride in the 90s, expanding its cast of characters and taking old ones in unexpected directions. Along the way, the little town of Springfield (a self-contained world with its own font!) became a miniature of the American scene and the Simpson family, more than ever, felt like us, besieged on all sides by dull and unrewarding jobs, mediocre media,[7] and familial discord.

Interest remained steady in Simpsonabilia, an interest that was met by the publication of *Simpsons Illustrated* magazine, *Simpsons* books, and the release of video games tailored to the die-hard fan. With the creation of the Bongo Comics Group and new, improved sets of trading cards, The Simpsons seemed to be everywhere once again. Screen savers and CD-ROMs brought the characters into the computer age and, thanks to industrious fans on the Internet, anyone could now sign off of their PC with a sound clip of Homer proclaiming, "You can kiss my curvy butt goodbye!" Probably not what Bill Gates had in mind.

Home Sweet Homer

After ten years, it's fair to ask if *The Simpsons* still retains the sense of risk and willingness to push the envelope that made it so appealing when it began. Happily, neither time nor success has mellowed its

approach nor blunted its wit. If *The Simpsons* has become an institution, it remains an innovative one. There is always a sense that the show is afraid of repeating itself and that a real effort has been made to continue to surprise and delight. It's part of why the show has legions of fans around the world who have responded by adopting

Bart and Lisa mugs.

Springfield as their own hometown. Viewers identify with this family because, with all their problems and imperfections, the Simpsons seem more realistic than most of their live-action competition.

Although they were in some ways a knowing pastiche of the TV families we'd grown up with (Springfield was also the name of the town in *Father Knows Best*, Homer's ever-present beard owes something to Fred Flintstone's five o' clock shadow, and Marge's necklace comes straight out of the Wilma Collection), The Simpsons were like no other family we'd ever seen. Never before had we seen a family that unashamedly spent so much time in front of the tube, nor had we ever seen

Advertisement for one of The Franklin Mint's collectible Simpson plates.

a show so willing to poke fun at the medium. Our frequent glimpses of the Simpsons' TV screen have, in fact, provided some of the show's most memorable satiric barbs.

If (as some critics have charged) TV Dads are bumbling and ineffectual, Homer is their worst nightmare, a father whose relationship with his own brain is casual at best. Everything he knows he's learned from television: he's the ultimate couch potato, the

Box of Topps' Simpsons candy containers from the U.K.

proud product of a lifetime of viewing. As such, Homer is the real baby of the family, insisting on instant gratification and bitterly disappointed when he doesn't get it. In Homer's world, the smallest problem is always a terrible crisis, while any real emergency escapes his notice. Everything about him is a comic exaggeration. Bestriding the town of Springfield like some bald colossus, he is its Gargantua, its Falstaff, its noble Quixote.[8] Murphy's Law in a too tight pair of pants, Homer is pure Appetite blindly gnawing its way towards the light, although that light is usually in the refrigerator.[9] Like Chaplin's Little Tramp, we love Homer partly because he is unabashedly vulgar. It's not that we love vulgarity so much, but it means that something of our humanity has survived the harsh glare of the Millennium. We love him for the same reason we love all the great clowns: when he fails, we see ourselves and laugh.[10]

While Bart may share some of Homer's values and, in fact, seems doomed to perpetuate the Simpson legacy, his natural skepticism about everything may save him yet. A cross between The Yellow Kid and Johnny Rotten disguised as Dennis The Menace, Bart is the latest in a long line of American bad boys that can be traced back to *Huckleberry Finn*.[11] His only real allegiance is to his favorite cartoon and comic book, which is as it should be. Neither as meek as best friend

Milhouse nor as cruel as bullies Dolph, Kearney, and Jimbo, Bart's mayhem is essentially harmless. It's more of an intellectual exercise for this pint-sized Professor Moriarty, pranks pulled for the sheer pleasure of seeing them work. Like every generation, Bart might not always be sure what he's protesting but intuitively understands that keeping the enemy confused is a good first step.[12]

Lisa, on the other hand, sees all too well how unfair the world is. (Merge Lisa and Bart together and you might get Abbie Hoffman.) A look around the family she was born into is proof enough of that. If Bart is a Homer in the making, Lisa reflects the patience and good sense of her mother, the long-suffering Marge. Lisa, like Bart, can't be pigeonholed. Although she plays the nerd to Bart's troublemaker, she's still enough of a kid to laugh at *The Itchy and Scratchy Show* and enjoy the latest issue of *Non-Threatening Boys*. She is, everyone acknowledges, the only member of the family who may actually (shudder) *succeed*, something wildly inconsistent with the history of the Simpson family. And yet, she doesn't hold the rest of the family in contempt the way that, say, Darlene did on *Roseanne*.[13] Instead, she accepts her plight with grace and uses her gifts for everyone's sake, not just her own.

Acceptance is the essence of harried homemaker Marge, whose tower of hair proclaims her motherly authority. She loves her "special little guy" when few others would be inclined to and sees past Homer's, uh, everything to find qualities that she values more than intelligence. Adversity is always met with the healing balm of gelatin (which seems appropriate for someone who resembles a walking dessert) and, in a sense, Marge is the gelatin of the family, holding the various canned fruits that constitute the Simpsons tightly together when they threaten to fall apart. Her belief that all things can be cured through dessert may not always be justified, but her faith in her family is.

At the swaddled heart of the show sits Maggie, a silent enigma. Like an Ivesian tone poem, Maggie refuses to yield her secrets. An odd, and perhaps unintentional, joke of the series has been that this seemingly most innocent member of the family may be its most sociopathic (and that's saying something in this household). She's attacked Homer with a hammer, shot Mr. Burns (with what some would consider extreme prejudice), and is engaged in a mysterious rivalry

Plaster Moulding Set from the U.K.

Promo poster for the "Who Shot Mr. Burns?" contest.

---

in its level of topicality and high standard of writing. How many other shows have been responsible for so many memorable lines? In addition, when it takes on subjects like rock music, fashion dolls, or vegetarianism, it gets them *right*. Like Homer attempting to rap (to the disdain of Bart and Lisa), too many programs have made the viewer groan by attempting to be self-consciously hip. *The Simpsons* never does this, which surely makes it an anomaly in the context of most network shows. If it sometimes seems to be cynical, it is also a show with a heart. I've seen it elicit both laughter and tears within the same five minutes. It also has a keen sense of its own history, something that delights attentive fans and also keeps the show from retreading too much old ground.

The Simpsons have become inextricably tangled up in our culture and not just our popular culture. A recent book by Michael Kinsley featured a blurb on the cover that compared the political pundit to none other than Bart Simpson. Scanning an essay on Franz Kafka the other day, I did a double take as the writer, arguing that Kafka's influence was not limited to so-called high culture, listed as his proof Charlie Chaplin, David Lynch, Terry Gilliam and...*The Simpsons*. Sometimes it's difficult to tell the difference between reality and Springfield.

with Baby Gerald, the baby with one eyebrow. I like to think that all of the qualities that set Homer, Marge, Bart, and Lisa apart are present in Maggie in an intensely concentrated amount and Springfield should consider itself lucky that she never gets any older.

What always links them together is that they don't fit in, they're all misfits, they're *Simpsons*. In many ways, they have no one to depend on but each other. Despite Homer's traditional throttling of "the boy," reminiscent of the hapless Isidore from Milt Gross' *Nize Baby* strip ("Mowriss, not in de had!"), the audience senses that each of them is joined together by something more profound than family ties. Muddling through with their limited equipment, the Simpsons have sworn a misfit oath of loyalty to support one another in the face of an increasingly mad and complex world and, when push comes to shove, they do exactly that.

You're Here Forever

Of course, *The Simpsons* is much more than the family that lends its name to the show. It boasts one of the largest supporting casts in television history and manages to lend each character some measure of individuality, thanks in large part to a remarkably talented group of vocal actors who seemed destined to work together. I still can't figure out how Homer's voice comes out of Dan Castellaneta, whereas Julie Kavner only needed to tweak her normal voice to arrive at Marge. Nancy Cartwright originally tried out for the part of Lisa, but discovered she had the perfect voice for a 10-year old boy. Yeardley Smith's voice fairly cries out for animation, while Hank Azaria brings an inspired nasality to some of Springfield's crankier residents like Moe the Bartender and Chief Wiggum.

Be the talk of your next slumber party with this fashionable nightshirt.

Harry Shearer and Phil Hartman are masters of the sincerely insincere, Shearer managing to alternate between both the menacing Mr. Burns and the obsequious Smithers (not to mention peppering the show with an endless stream of media personalities), and Hartman providing memorable con men like Lionel Hutz and Troy McClure.

Another secret of the show's success over the years is that it has never talked down to its audience. *The Simpsons* remains unique

Homer and Lisa squirt rings from the U.K.

On the network news the evening that I write this, the anchorman went to commercial by crowing about their next scoop, "Aluminum Foil: 50 Years Old Today!" You half expect to look up and see Kent Brockman in the anchor chair.

This is really what *The Simpsons* is all about: reflecting our own world back to us in stretchable putty, making it seem both familiar and surreal. It looks like our world, it has many of the same cities and celebrities, but there's some crucial differences. Everyone's hands only have four fingers, for a start. And there's an almost global sense of amnesia about the numerous times that various Simpson family members have become high-profile celebrities, only to disappear swiftly into anonymity once more. They do it simply because it's time to tell another story. The citizens of Springfield, a town which is everywhere and nowhere,[14] comprise an acting troupe whose job it is to absorb our common experience and then paint it yellow. Maybe we're living in Shelbyville, that nearby town whose residents are all strange doppelgangers of the people who live in Springfield. Or maybe, as Salman Rushdie said of Oz, maybe we have become Springfield.

The laws of this alternate universe are merciless and unchanging. There may be sweeping changes in it but when the 30 minutes are up, all the players will be back where they began, swept back into place like tenpins in some cosmic Bowl-A-Rama. Homer will come no closer to succeeding this week than he did this last week. Marge's Candide-like faith will be restored once more. Bart and Lisa will continue to laugh at Itchy and Scratchy, little suspecting that they, too, are indestructible. Mr. Burns can harass Homer but never destroy him. Like some Beckettian tramp in his own *Waiting For Go-D'oh!*, Homer waits patiently for a dream that does not come. His innate sense of doofusy beatitude is what saves him from despair as he proves the truth of the late Charles Bukowski's maxim that "the luck of the fool is inviolate."[15]

For even as The Simpsons lose, they win. Stumbling blissfully week after week into preordained failure only to emerge unscathed,[16]

so shall you and I take that final pratfall as we go back to the drawing board to await the hand that animates us. And it is in that elysian field, dear friends, that land filled with mountains of sugar and oceans of beer, that happy land of chocolate dogs and pressed peanut sweepings, that land in which the sky rains donuts and each man is his own king, that we will no longer have to fear the sulfuric cocktails and frantic hatchets of mortality, the itch and scratch of our day-to-day banality. On that day, with the shorts finally eaten and the cow, at long last, had, we will no longer be *I* but *Karumba*,[17] woo-hooing down the corridors of Time as the heavens part to reveal our true name and we dash through the garage door of Infinity, seeking once again our own place on the couch even as we fear what it will do to us.

All right, let me put it another way. To paraphrase what a woman once wrote about the work of novelist Laurence Sterne, beware of telling me that you do not love *The Simpsons*, for I fear I will love you less.

Robert W. Getz
October, 1997
Springfield, U.S.A.

Endnotes

[1] In the liner notes for *Songs In The Key Of Springfield*, Matt Groening writes, "I wanted a big, fully orchestrated, obnoxious, arrogant theme that promised you the best time of your life." Danny Elfman was the perfect composer to provide it. By transferring the off-kilter rhythms of his band *Oingo Boingo* to Film and TV music, Elfman became one of the few modern film composers whose style, an odd melange of Raymond Scott and Bernard Herrmann, was as instantly recognizable as John Williams. The frantic theme that drives the "Breakfast Machine" sequence in *Pee-Wee's Big Adventure* (directed by Tim Burton, 1985) is worth the price of admission alone. Other collaborations with Burton are also noteworthy, including *Beetlejuice* (1988), *Batman* (1989), *Edward Scissorhands* (1990), and *The Nightmare Before Christmas* (1993).

[2] It's telling, perhaps, that this is also a pretty good description of the viewpoint to be found in the work of one of Groening's idols, late rock iconoclast Frank Zappa.

[3] Many of the other names on the show (Flanders, Kearney, Lovejoy and Quimby) come from streets in Portland, Oregon, where Groening grew up. His mother's maiden name was Wiggum. ("47 Secrets About The Simpsons, A Poem Of Sorts, And Some Filler," *Bartman* # 4.)

[4] The obvious pun on the traditional Japanese Noh play, however, will not be made here by me. Besides which, there's a much worse one coming up later.

[5] One of the most famous controversies surrounding *The Simpsons* was the outrage created by the "Underachiever—And Proud Of It, Man!" T-shirts. Some school officials were so threatened by them that they banned them from the classroom. Matt Groening would later explain, "The point of that T-shirt was that no kids call themselves underachievers—that's a label grown-ups slap on kids. And the proper wisenheimer response to being labeled an underachiever, of course, is to be 'proud of it, man!' " (*Bartman and Radioactive Man* #1).

[6] The merchandising of *The Simpsons* presents something of a paradox. How do you merchandise a product that is, in part, dedicated to satirizing consumer culture? In at least one instance, the show got to have its cake and eat it when they had the talking Bart Simpson doll say, "Kids In TV Land, You're Being Duped!" The characters have also each gotten a chance to poke fun at the Simpsons juggernaut: Lisa tells the creator of Malibu Stacy that she'd be mortified if anyone ever produced an inferior product "with the Simpson name on it." *Mad* magazine, which (along with the old Jay Ward cartoons) could be considered a comedic midwife to *The Simpsons*, found itself in a similar situation. Their solution was to talk about whatever they were selling in the most self-deprecating terms possible. And, of course, *Mad* had the ultimate anti-consumer line (a line that still makes me laugh today) when it would happily and regularly end a sales pitch with, "But mainly, go kill yourself!"

[7] One of the show's great jokes is that the ultra-violent McBain movies are nothing more than Itchy and Scratchy cartoons for adults.

[8] There is also a Homer Simpson in Nathanael West's novel, *The Day Of The Locust*. For more on this topic, see my letter in *Simpsons Comics* #9.

[9] Deep in my own pork fried, cathode rayed heart, I have to admit that when I look into the Abyss I see Homer Simpson staring back at me and confess that his lust for Moon Waffles is also my own. I doubt that even Homer would admit to the Grilled Chocolate Sandwich I had not long ago. All right, the two Grilled Chocolate Sandwiches.

[10] Homer also has something of the sweet, befuddled charm of Warner Brothers contract player Hugh Herbert, whose dizzy monologues were frequently interspersed with his trademark "Woo woo!"

[11] Groening relates how part of the impetus for creating the anarchic Bart was a deep disappointment in how the promise of the whirling tornado that graced the credits of the *Dennis The Menace* TV program seemed betrayed by the relatively clean-scrubbed and well-behaved Jay North. "But I never forgot that primal thrill of seeing the little cartoon tornado...I filed that moment away..." ("The Hitherto Untold Secret Origin Of A Certain Notorious Spiky-Haired Cartoon Character," *Simpsons Comics* # 20). Like Dennis, Bart is also supplied with a slingshot. Lisa hits the nail on the head when she refers to Bart as a "vile burlesque of irrepressible youth." The show eventually did an explicit parody when George Bush moved in across the street from the Simpsons and played Mr. Wilson to Bart's Dennis.

[12] Another spiritual antecedent for Bart could be Bart Collins, the boy protagonist of the film *The 5000 Fingers Of Dr. T* (1953). Written by Dr. Seuss, the story is an elaborate fantasy in which Bart imagines his piano teacher (whose last name, Terwilliker, is awfully close to that of the other Bart's greatest nemesis, Sideshow Bob Terwilliger) to be the master of an enormous facility in which small boys have their toys confiscated and are forced to practice the piano. Anticipating his namesake, Bart throws a monkey wrench into things by inventing a device that steals sound from out of the air. Triumphant, he leads the gleeful group in a cacophonous version of "Chopsticks." The outstretched yellow hands that sit atop the boys' "Happy Fingers" beanies look eerily like they've come from a bunch of Bart Simpson dolls. Some rough beast slouching towards Springfield to be born?

[13] It's interesting to note that the two most subversive sitcoms of the '90s, *The Simpsons* and *Roseanne*, both featured hard luck, blue collar families that celebrated their own dysfunction. Both were a million miles from the Reagan years of *Dallas* and *Dynasty*. Not surprisingly, Roseanne is a big fan of *The Simpsons* and listed it among her "Things To Be Thankful For" on a 1997 *Oprah Winfrey* show.

[14] The show takes great pains not to identify Springfield with any actual town. (Woe betide the earnest young newbie who proudly proclaims to a Simpsons Internet newsgroup that he has discovered the "true" location of Springfield. Suffice it to say that the pain and humiliation that follows is slightly less uncomfortable than slamming one's fingers in a car door.) Springfield is also timeless, a place where the ages of the Simpsons remain constant even as the years swirl about them. This free-floating chronology often seems to confuse the Simpsons themselves.

[15] Here the author is parading a vague sort of erudition in an attempt to distract you (and himself) from the fact that he's really talking about grown-ups collecting toys. There's no need for him to feel ashamed about this. There are actually people who watch *The Wizard Of Oz* using Pink Floyd's *Dark Side Of The Moon* as a soundtrack. Keeping this in mind is a pretty good way to keep from feeling bad about anything.

[16] Woo hoo!

[17] *Karumba*, i.e., All-World-Mind. See *Homer And The Unconscious*, Duntov Hakow-Mann.

A Short Word On Collecting

It started out harmless enough at first: a doll here, an action figure there. I've got the sort of pack rat mentality that would rather bring something home than leave it behind. With *The Simpsons*, I can remember that there was a time early on when I wondered why there wasn't any merchandise available to buy (which gives you some idea how long ago this was). When it began to appear, I didn't buy every single thing that came down the yellow pike, either: I liked the dolls and figures the best (and probably still do) and even though I didn't consider myself a Simpsons Collector *per se*, I had to admit that the stuff was starting to pile up.

Slowly, those bits of Springfieldian esoterica that didn't seem all that important at first started to look better and better somehow (*Say, how come I've never bought myself any of that Bart Simpson Hair Gel?*). I began to notice when shops would put Simpsons stuff in their Clearance aisle. I started to make inquiries and haunt collectible shops. People would stop to whisper and point when I walked by, barely able to suppress a whispered *Aye Caramba!* Eventually, I could no longer deny the truth: I was a Simpsons Collector, a Bart Addict, a Yellow Fiend.

The Simpsons has been such a pervasive presence that it's often been difficult to keep track of all the merchandise inspired by it. One would be just as likely to find some Simpsons item in a bakery or gift store as much as in a toy shop. These days, Simpsons items are produced very selectively with the recent emphasis being on more solid, upscale items like plates, salt and pepper shakers, and cookie jars. As for toys, there aren't that many being produced now in the United States. For many of the toys pictured here, you have to do some digging in the secondary market. Flea markets and shops that specialize in collectibles and magazines that cater to the serious collector are the best places to look. If you can make your wants known to as many dealers as possible, you increase the chances that they'll think of you when they come across something Simpsony.

In addition, the Internet offers many toy and collectible auctions that may help you in finding what you seek, not to mention a whole world of enthusiastic collectors who'd be interested in hearing from you. If you can make contact with a dealer with access to overseas merchandise, so much the better. *The Simpsons* is an international hit and there are lots of items (especially edible ones) that were never produced in the U.S. Sometimes the collectibles will come to you: In 1997, Vivid Imaginations in the U.K. produced an enviable line of dolls, keychains, magnets, and pencil toppers. Some of these found their way to Suncoast Video stores in the U.S. as part of their promotion of the *Simpsons* video set.

One of the humbling aspects of doing a project like this, of course, is that just when you think you've caught the lay of the land, you discover that the horizon is somewhat broader than you'd imagined. Although I know I've missed items (I think it would be difficult not to when dealing with a phenomenon as popular as *The Simpsons*), I think that the guide as a whole provides a good overview of what kinds of collectibles are available. One notable exception, however, is T-shirts. No TV show has inspired more T-shirts than *The Simpsons*, but I've virtually ignored them here. Their status as a "collectible" seems to me a little hazy, so I've left that question for another day (or perhaps, more patient hands). Other items were the victims of judgment calls or last minute difficulties. I'd be very interested in hearing from readers who would like to bring any neglected pieces to my attention. Please write to me care of the publisher or you can send your e-mail to rgetz@hotmail.com.

The prices I've provided range from the least you can expect to pay for an item (not mint but still in some sort of collectible condition) to that same item in mint condition. They're based both on prices that I myself have paid, as well as prices I have seen posted throughout the secondary market by dealers in advertisements or in collectible shops. Keep in mind that no prices are written in stone when it comes to collectibles. You may find someone asking more than the median price suggested here or, perhaps, less. It's always up to what that particular dealer thinks something is worth and/or how quickly he or she wants to sell it. The prices here aspire to provide collectors with a good general idea of what is being asked for these collectibles in today's market.

Finally, it's always difficult to predict what will or won't become a valuable collectible and so the best rule of thumb is always to buy what you love. The hordes of investors who appeared out of nowhere to bag and board comic books in the belief that they'd become valuable forgot a crucial bit of information: *Superman* #1 is valuable because so few of them were saved. When millions of collectors all save the same thing, the chances are slim that it will increase in value. Judge what something is worth to *you*. Another rule: as a grizzled old prospector once told me, "You never regret what you buy, only what you don't buy." There are no truer words than this. We'd need another book for me to tell you about all the times I decided to "think about" something and come back later, only to be disappointed. In the dark Kwik-E-Mart of my soul, I still long for that Bart Simpson joystick I could have had. Like some spiky-headed Maltese Falcon, it haunts my dreams and turns my days into waking nightmares.

Don't say I didn't warn you.

Chapter One: Dolls/Figures

One of the easiest and most enjoyable ways to begin a Simpsons collection is simply to pick from the vast number of dolls and figures the characters have inspired. If you've picked up this book you probably already have the Burger King dolls. They're easy to find, a nice size and will remind you of your collection's humble start years after you've filled your home with Simpsons paraphernalia (that is your intention, isn't it?). Almost as ubiquitous are the Jesco Bendies, bendable figures that were available separately or as a set. The camping figures produced by Burger King are also fairly easy to track down, although the cardboard backgrounds that came with them are becoming difficult to find.

Bart is, obviously, the easiest Simpson figure to find. It's difficult to negotiate the length and breadth of any flea market worthy of the name without running into him. I don't think it's an exaggeration to say that Bart Simpson has become the Mickey Mouse of the late 20th century. His face, as you'll see, has been merchandised in countless ways. In some ways, then, it's more satisfying and challenging to collect sets that include the entire family. The series produced by Presents is a good example. Similar to the Burger King dolls, the set includes two Bart figures, one with slingshot, one without. These came in two different sizes with the smaller size being harder to find. The Dan Dee "Special Expressions" rag dolls and "Collectible Figures" are also desirable family sets.

A favorite of mine is the German Kinder Egg set of Simpsons. Arguably the smallest Simpson figures, each figure sits on a section of couch which fits together with the others. Perhaps the fan favorite is the set of action figures produced by Mattel. Each figure comes with a plastic word balloon into which you can place 1 of 5 different sayings. The set includes a Nelson figure, one of the few non-family *Simpsons* figures to have been produced (Others include the Grampa Simpson

figure in the *3-D Chess Set*, the Krusty The Clown doll, and the Ned Flanders figure from the Australian Milky Way set). A *Sofa And Boob Tube* package completes the Mattel set.

More recently, the folks at Treasure Craft responsible for the Bart and Homer cookie jars have come out with two sets of salt and pepper shakers which, together, make up the whole family, complete with couch and TV. These are occasional and welcome exceptions in the U.S., however, and not the rule. Most Simpson figures now seem to come from abroad and American fans will have to do a little bit of work to get hold of many of the wonderful pieces that have recently appeared in the U.K. and elsewhere.

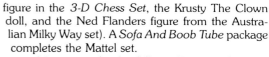

Lisa Simpson rag doll. Dan Dee. Its original card is identical to the one on the "Special Expressions" doll (see below). Uncarded $3-5, Carded $7-10.

Above: The unofficial gargoyle of every flea market: The Great Yellow Underachiever. This small Bart Simpson rag doll from Dan Dee, here uncarded, is one of the most common Simpson collectibles. Its original card is identical to the one on the "Special Expressions" doll (see below). Uncarded $3-5, Carded $7-10.

Bart Simpson stick-on doll. Dan Dee. Add suction cups to the hands and feet of the rag doll and throw in a decorated shirt and—voila!—you've got the Bart Stick-On doll. $4-8.

Bart Simpson coin bank. Dan Dee. This bank also came with an orange or blue shirt. $6-10.

Bart Simpson rag doll. Dan Dee. This rag doll, which features a plastic head, comes in two versions. The first has a smaller head with black lines drawn around the ears and mouth, while the other's head is larger and flared with no decoration. The flared head appears to be identical to the one on the Valentine's Day doll (see below). $4-8.

Bart Simpson valentine doll. Dan Dee. What ardent suitor could fail with this expression of affection? Cooties, man! $6-10.

One can't help but wonder what some 23rd century archaeologist will make of this frightening tableau. *Bart longa, vita brevis.* Bart banks from Street Kids. $3-5.

Bart Simpson clip-on. Dan Dee. $5-8.

Bart Simpson rag doll from Dan Dee. This large, boxed version of the Bart rag doll features plastic eyes. $10-15.

Bartman clip-on. Dan Dee. $5-8

This Lisa Simpson rag doll originally came boxed. Dan Dee. Large, with plastic eyes. $10-15.

Talking Bart Simpson doll. Dan Dee. Once a fairly common item, this talking doll is becoming harder to find in good condition. With six "smart-aleck sayings." $40-$60.

Maggie Simpson rag doll. Dan Dee. Large, with plastic eyes. $8-12.

Fuzzy arcade Bart, large. Acme Premium. The largest of the stuffed Barts. $10-15. The large Homer and Marge Acme dolls are much harder to find and command prices in the $40-60 range when you can find them.

Fabric arcade Bart, small, from Acme Premium. The Simpson dolls produced by Acme were generally found as prizes in arcades or fairgrounds. $8-12.

Top left: Homer Simpson "Special Expressions" rag doll from Dan Dee. Homer's bowling shirt features the logo for "Barney's Bowlarama" prominently on the back. $8-12.

Top center: Marge Simpson "Special Expressions" rag doll. Dan Dee. $8-12.

Top right: Bart Simpson "Special Expressions" rag doll. Dan Dee. This version of the small Bart rag doll features a gold jacket and a green "Special Expressions" tag. $8-12.

Bottom center: Lisa Simpson "Special Expressions" rag doll. Dan Dee. This version features a pink jacket. Note the sibling rivalry going on between Bart and Lisa inside the word balloons. $8-12.

Bottom right: Maggie Simpson "Special Expressions" rag doll. Dan Dee. $8-12.

Homer Simpson "Collectible Figure" from Dan Dee. Like the "Special Expressions" doll, the shirt this Homer wears also features the logo for "Barney's Bowlarama" on the back. $8-12.

Marge Simpson "Collectible Figure." Dan Dee. $8-12.

Bart Simpson "Collectible Figure." Dan Dee. $8-12.

Lisa Simpson "Collectible Figure."
Dan Dee. $8-12.

Maggie Simpson "Collectible
Figure." Dan Dee. $8-12.

Homer Simpson action figure from Mattel. Isn't a Homer action figure an oxymoron? With five "fatherly phrases," helmet, glove, and isotope. $12-16.

Opposite page:
Top left: Lisa Simpson action figure. Mattel. With five "phrases to bug brothers" and saxophone. $15-18.

Top right: Maggie Simpson action figure. Mattel. With five "thoughts to suck on" and kiddie scooter. $15-18.

Bottom left: Bartman action figure. Mattel. With five "warnings for evildoers," cape and slingshot. $12-16.

Bottom right: Nelson action figure. Mattel. With five "wisecracks" and garbage can. Now you can take your revenge on Springfield's most notorious bully. It's your turn to laugh and point at Nelson or dress him like a tool. $12-16.

Bart Simpson action figure. Mattel. With five "cool things to say" and skateboard. $12-16.

Marge Simpson action figure. Mattel. With five "things moms say," apron, and cookie tray. $12-16.

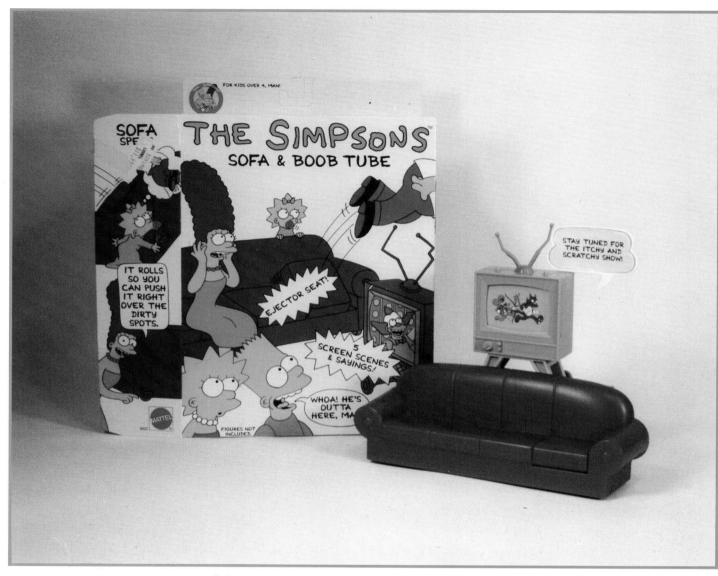

Sofa And Boob Tube set. Mattel. Created to accompany the Mattel action figures, the sofa features an ejector seat, while the television comes with five pictures and five captions. $25-30.

Bart action wind-up, red,
from Mattel. $8-12.

Bart action wind-up, green,
from Mattel. $8-12.

Lisa action wind-up. Mattel. $8-12.

Maggie action wind-up. Mattel. $8-12.

Homer water squirter. Mattel. $6-10.

Bart water squirter. Mattel. $6-10.

Bart (with scuba gear) water squirter. Mattel. $6-10.

Maggie water squirter. Mattel. $6-10.

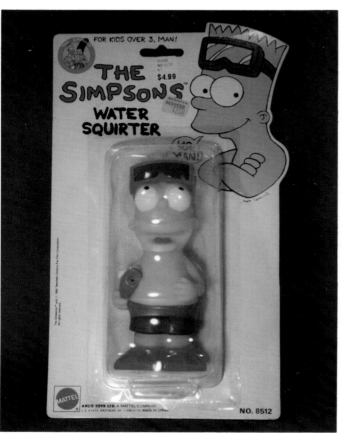

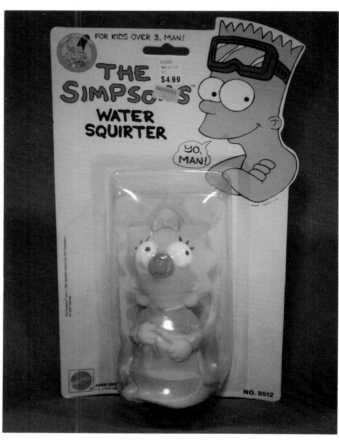

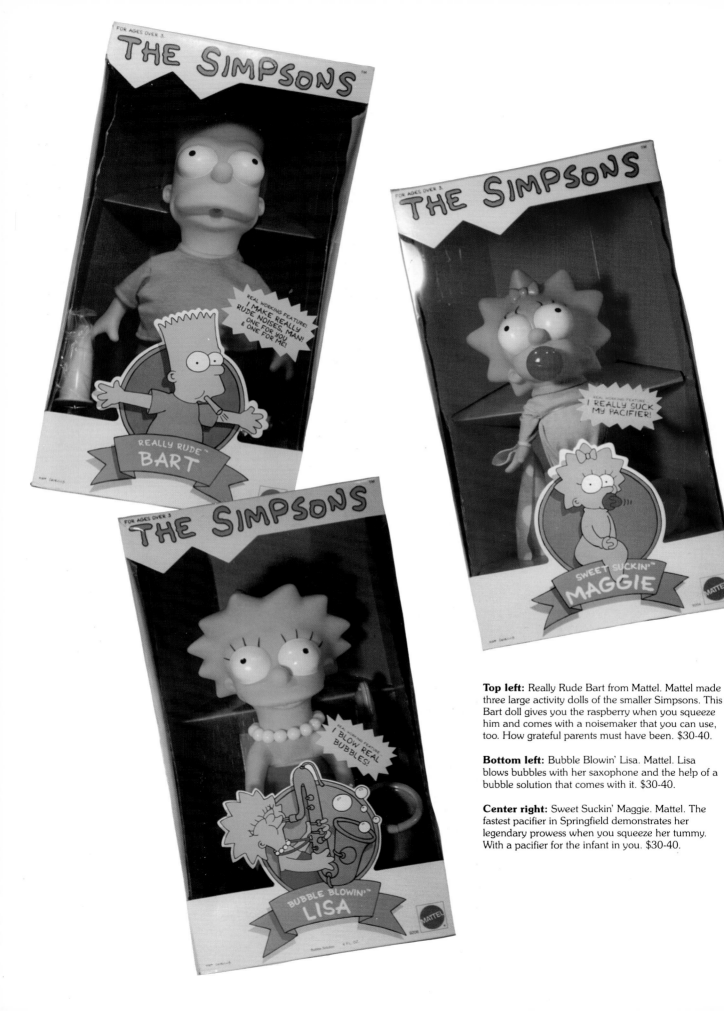

Top left: Really Rude Bart from Mattel. Mattel made three large activity dolls of the smaller Simpsons. This Bart doll gives you the raspberry when you squeeze him and comes with a noisemaker that you can use, too. How grateful parents must have been. $30-40.

Bottom left: Bubble Blowin' Lisa. Mattel. Lisa blows bubbles with her saxophone and the help of a bubble solution that comes with it. $30-40.

Center right: Sweet Suckin' Maggie. Mattel. The fastest pacifier in Springfield demonstrates her legendary prowess when you squeeze her tummy. With a pacifier for the infant in you. $30-40.

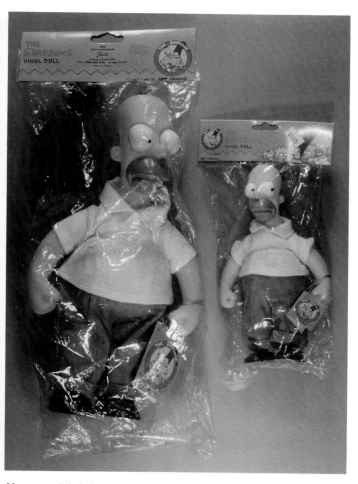

Homer vinyl dolls, large and small, from Presents. It's either Homer or Popeye has really let himself go. Large, $12-15. Small, $8-12.

Marge vinyl dolls. Presents. The kids will have hours of fun reenacting their favorite scenes from *The Bride Of Frankenstein* with these lovable dolls. The Malibu Stacy of an alternate universe. Large, $12-15. Small, $8-12.

Bart vinyl dolls. Presents. Large, $12-15. Small, $8-12.

Bart (with slingshot) vinyl dolls. Presents. Large, $12-15. Small, $8-12.

Maggie vinyl doll, large. Presents. Although I've yet to see it, I'll assume that a smaller edition exists. Large, $12-15.

Lisa vinyl dolls. Presents. Large, $12-15. Small, $8-12.

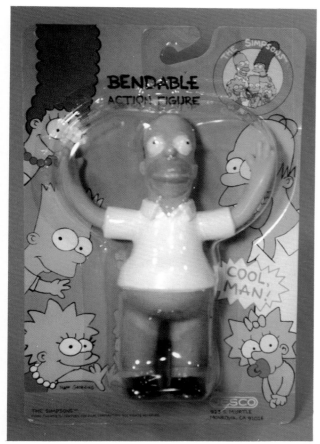

Homer Simpson bendie from Jesco. Like Homer himself, the only way this doll can't bend is from the waist. Originally released in 1990, the Homer and Bart bendies reappeared in 1997, carded by Vivid Imaginations in the U.K. but with the "Jesco" logo still on the figures. $5-8.

Marge Simpson bendie. Jesco. $5-8.

Bart Simpson bendie. Jesco. $5-8.

Lisa Simpson bendie. Jesco. $5-8.

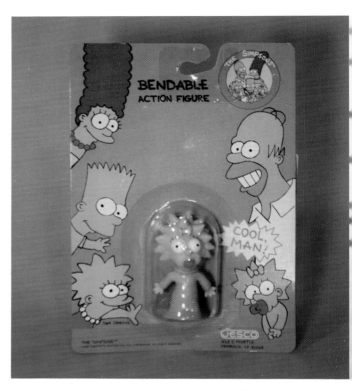

Maggie Simpson bendie. Jesco. $5-8.

Simpson family bendie set. Jesco. $30-35.

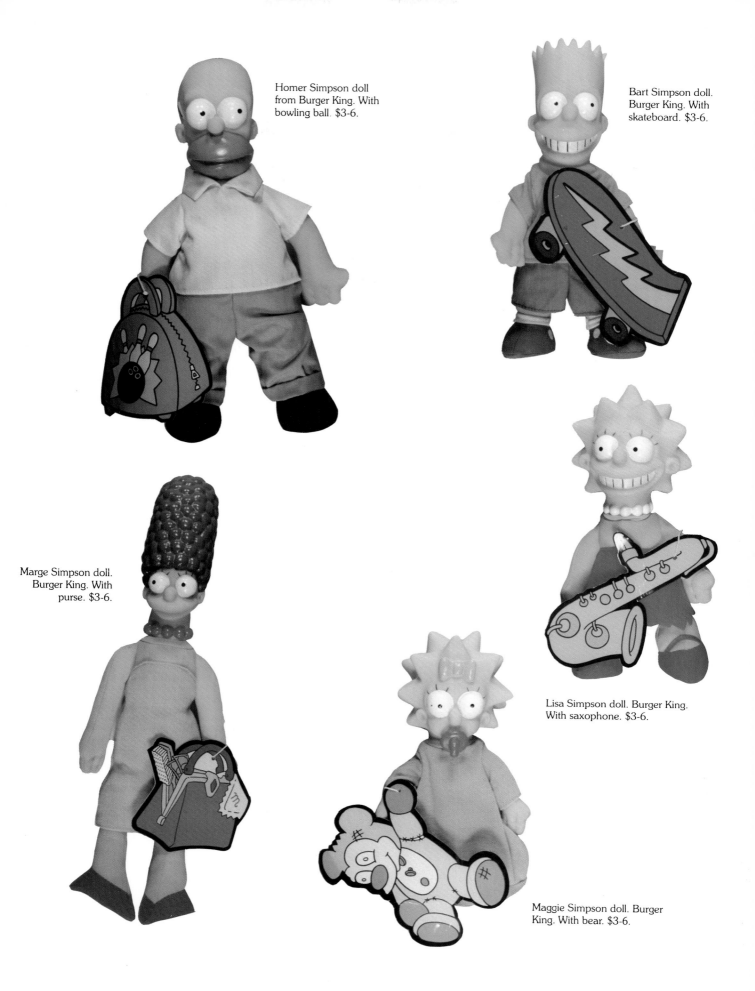

Homer Simpson doll from Burger King. With bowling ball. $3-6.

Bart Simpson doll. Burger King. With skateboard. $3-6.

Marge Simpson doll. Burger King. With purse. $3-6.

Lisa Simpson doll. Burger King. With saxophone. $3-6.

Maggie Simpson doll. Burger King. With bear. $3-6.

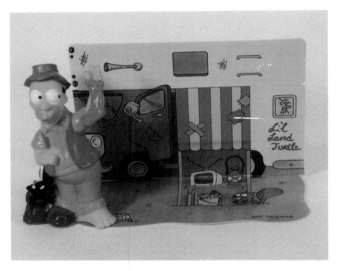

Homer Simpson figure from Burger King. Each of the figures in this series depicted the Simpsons roughing it in the great outdoors. The figure was accompanied by a cardboard background. Although the figures themselves are fairly common, it's difficult to find the backgrounds. Figure, $2-5. With background, $7-10.

Marge Simpson figure. Burger King. $2-5. With background, $7-10.

Bart Simpson figure. Burger King. $2-5. With background, $7-10.

Lisa Simpson figure. Lisa does some woodshedding. Burger King. $2-5. With background, $7-10.

Maggie Simpson figure. Burger King. $2-5. With background, $7-10.

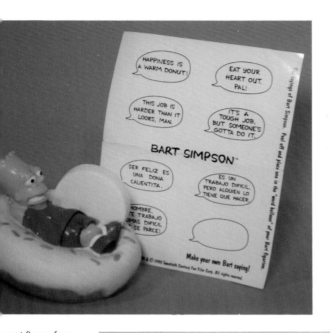

...onut figure from
...ell's Donuts. The
...ar donut chain
...d this relaxed
...g Bart with
...s in English and
...sh. $3-5.

Homer donut figure.
Winchell's. $3-5.

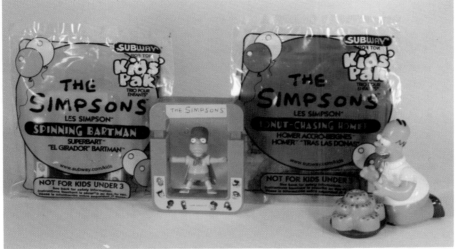

Spinning Bartman and
Donut-Chasing Homer
from Subway. $1-3 each.

Bart and Lisa wheeled figures from Burger King, U.K. $5-8
each.

...al Lisa and Skateboarding Bart from Subway. $1-3 each.

Homer with football PVC, large and small. $3-6 each.

Maggie with ice cream and Lisa PVCs. $3-6 each.

Marge with Snowball II PVC, large and small. $3-6 each.

Bart plays air guitar PVC, large and small. Small figure has "Spraitbach Germany" label. $3-6 each.

Bart on skateboard PVC, large and small. The small one has a label that reads "Spraitbach Germany." $3-6 each.

Krusty The Clown doll from Play by Play. Make sure it isn't set for "Evil." $10-15.

Bart bean bag. Jemini, France. $8-12.

Marge bean bag from Jemini. France. $8-12.

Lisa bean bag. Jemini, France. $8-12.

Marge cling-on. Yapon,
Sweden. $10-15.

Homer cling-on from Yapon. Sweden. $10-15.

Bart cling-on. Yapon,
Sweden. $10-15.

Maggie cling-on. Yapon,
Sweden. $10-15.

Lisa cling-on. Yapon, Sweden. $10-15.

Bart with striped shirt. Jemini,
France. $8-12.

Plastic Bart bank
from Miniland,
Spain. $15-20.

Marge, Bart, and Homer ceramic figurines from Harry James, U.K. $12-15 each.

Bartman ceramic figurine. Harry James, U.K. $12-15.

Bart ceramic bank from Tropico, France. $12-15.

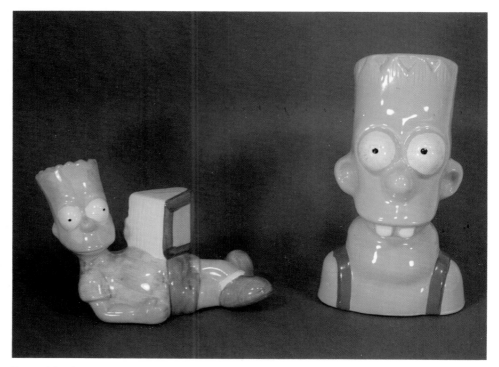

Bart with book ceramic bank, U.K. Harry James? $15-20. Unlicensed Bart ceramic bank, U.K. Looks more like Cletus if you ask me. $10-15.

Bart, Maggie, Homer and Marge, and Lisa figurines from Topfair, U.K. $8-12 each.

Homer and Bart Sofa Buddies figurine from Vivid Imaginations, U.K. $20-25.

Simpsons snowglobe/stamper set from Noteworthy, Canada. Bart, Bartman, Bart with skateboard, and Lisa and Maggie. These small figures doubled as rubber stamps when you removed the base. $10-15 set.

Bart and Bartman snowglobes from Convert, France. $8-12 each.

Lisa and Maggie snowglobes. Convert, France. $8-12 each.

Simpsons bell jar figurine from The Franklin Mint. $30-40.

Homer, Bart, and Marge figures created to promote Vizir Detergent, Belgium. The Vizir logo can be seen...

...as displayed here. It's possible that these figures were never officially released. $15-20 each.

Christmas ornaments. This six-piece set originally appeared as pencil toppers (see Marge pencil), but were later recycled as ornaments. $8-12 set.

Simpson family set from Mars Confectionery, Australia. To collect this eight piece set, you had to buy a "Lucky Dip" box which contained a Milky Way bar and a "mystery toy" or Simpsons figure. The ratio of mystery toys to Simpsons figures was roughly 6 to 1, so a complete set wasn't easy to put together. Slightly bigger than the Kinder Egg set. $30-40 set.

Simpson family set from Kinder Eggs, Germany. Each of the five pieces in this set came inside a chocolate egg. $20-25 set.

Bart with red or yellow car from Arco, U.K. $7-10.

Maggie and Homer with car. Arco, U.K. $7-10.

Prototype figures from unknown animation house, possibly for Jesco bendies. Modeling compound. $75-100 each.

Bart in Itchy and Scratchy T-shirt from Vivid Imaginations, U.K. This doll (and the three that follow) was also available in France from Tropico uncarded but with a tag that reproduced the card art. $20-30.

Bart in Krusty T-shirt. Vivid Imaginations, U.K. $20-30.

Don Homer in Hawaiian outfit. Vivid Imaginations, U.K. $20-30.

Homer as Nature intended him. What a piece of work is Man! Vivid Imaginations, U.K. $20-30.

No Simpsons guide would be complete without at least one of the numerous and legendary Tijuana bootleg Barts. Note how the part of Bart's head seen above the hat seems to bear no relation to the part below it. Que lastima! $12-15.

Bart standee from Starmakers. $3-6.

Homer and Marge standee. Starmakers. $3-6.

Simpsons standee. Starmakers. $3-6.

6 ft. Bart Simpson stand-up.
Starmakers. $20-25.

Chapter Two: Homer's Bathroom

(Soaps, Shampoos, Beauty Supplies)

Homer Simpson bubble bath from Cosrich. $5-8.

Marge Simpson bubble bath. Cosrich. $5-8.

Bart Simpson bubble bath. Cosrich. $5-8.

Lisa Simpson bubble bath. Cosrich. $5-8.

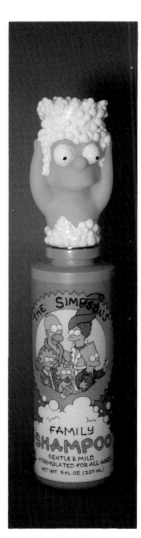

Homer Simpson family
shampoo. Cosrich. $5-8.

Marge Simpson family
shampoo. Cosrich. $5-8.

Bart Simpson family
shampoo. Cosrich. $5-8.

Lisa Simpson family
shampoo. Cosrich. $5-8.

Maggie Simpson family
shampoo. Cosrich. $5-8.

Bart Simpson bubble bath from Grosvenor, U.K. $8-12.

Bart Simpson bath gel from Euromark, U.K. $10-15.

Soap dish and bath plug sets from
Euromark, U.K. $10-15 each.

Bart Simpson bath soap from Cosrich. $5-8.

Bart Simpson battery operated
toothbrush with timer stand from
Helm Toy. $7-10.

Toothbrush sets from Maxill. Canada. Homer/Marge and Bart/Lisa, $3-6 each.

Lisa Simpson Puffa Pal from Odd Ball, U.K. An asthma inhaler cover! Homer and Bart also available. $12-15.

Bart Simpson finger paint gel soap and Radical Hair Stuff styling gel for that spiky look from Cosrich. $5-8 each.

Marge's Beauty Bag from Mattel. This collection of elegant toiletries advertises the large activity Simpsons dolls (*Really Rude Bart*, etc.) on the back. $12-15.

Simpsons adhesive bandages from Quantasia. $4-7.

Chapter Three: Marge's Kitchen

(Food, Cups, Plates, Cookie Jars)

Bowl and plate set from Tropico, France. $30-35 set.

Bart bowl and mug from Tropico, France. $25-30 each.

Milk chocolate breakfast set from Kinnerton, U.K. The mug and egg cup packaged together in this British set each originally contained a milk chocolate egg. $25-40.

Bart eggcup from Tropico, France. $20-25.

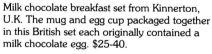

Homer and Marge mugs from One Of The Bunch. $8-12 each.

The classic Bart catchphrases preserved in convenient mug form. One Of The Bunch. $8-12 each.

Simpson family mug. The familiar logo appeared on the reverse of these One Of The Bunch mugs. $8-12.

"No Way, Man!" and "Over-achiever" mugs from Presents. $8-12 each.

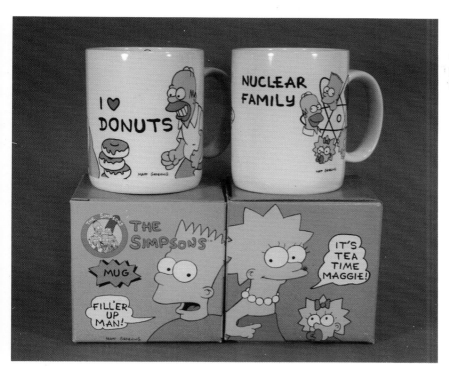

"I Love Donuts" and "Nuclear Family" mugs from Presents. $8-12 each.

Bart and Marge mugs, U.K. Rodelco. $8-12 each.

20 oz. Super mug. Blue plastic. $5-8

Frosty mug. Manufacturer
unknown. $8-12.

"Summer With The Simpsons" plastic jug from
Church's Chicken. $8-12.

Winchell's Donuts 45th Anniversary cup with
Homer, the best pitchman donuts ever had,
with the possible exception of *Twin Peaks'*
Special Agent Dale Cooper. Plastic. $4-7.

Two of the plastic cups produced by Burger King as part of their Simpsons promotion. Like the small BK figures, the cups picture the Simpsons in the woods. There were four cups in the complete set. Each cup $3-6.

Helping to hype the mystery of the "Who Shot Mr. Burns?" cliffhanger, 7-11 stores offered four large Big Gulp cups. Each cup, $2-5.

Big Gulp cups, same as above.

Subway invited their customers to "Homer-size" their drinks with this large cup. Do you dare accept the challenge? $2-4.

Kids' Pak bags from Subway's 1997 Simpsons promotion. With eco-friendly tips from Lisa on the back. $1-3.

Burger King placemat. $1-3.

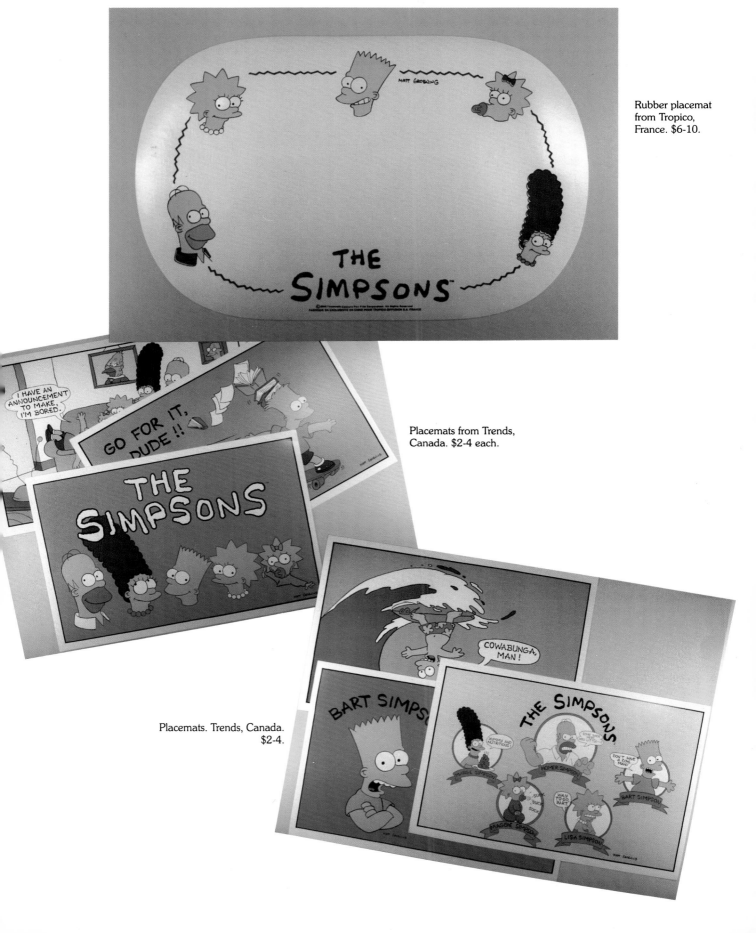

Rubber placemat
from Tropico,
France. $6-10.

Placemats from Trends,
Canada. $2-4 each.

Placemats. Trends, Canada.
$2-4.

Imagine how you'll impress your guests when they sit down to your fine china, your good silver...

...and your Bart Simpson hors d'oeuvres knives. Give them something to talk about as they wait for you to bring out those delicious steamed hams. From Tropico, France. $15-20.

Party assortment. Party cups, napkins and gift wrap from Chesapeake. $4-6 each. Party invitations from Gibson. $3-5. "Party Time" plates from Deeko, U.K. $3-5.

Party bags from Deeko, U.K. $3-6.

Party packs from Incoarte, Brazil. Stand-ups, favor
bags, and plates, $5-8 each.

Maggie Simpson one-year old
birthday candle. Wilton. $3-6.

Decorative cake candles from Wilton. Wilton was also responsible for a
set of Simpsons cookie cutters. $3-6.

Maggie Simpson plastic nursers from Binky.
$3-6 each.

Baby Bart plastic nursers. Binky. $3-6.

Hungry, but not in the mood for shorts? Then how about a brimming bowl of Simpsons Pasta Shapes, with each member of the family magically transformed into macaroni? This hearty lunch was available in the U.K. Also pictured is the lunch mug that was made available. Pasta Shapes from HP, $5-9, Pasta mug, $8-12.

Another cheesy Simpsons product. Macaroni and cheese from Kraft Foods, Australia. Mmmmm, non-fat milk solids... $7-10.

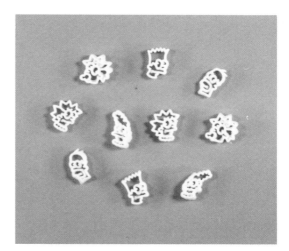

Some of the Simpsons macaronis.

Bart Bites from Burton's, U.K. Eat my biscuits! $4-8.

Homewheat Plain Chocolate Digestive from McVitie's, U.K. These British wafers featured a Simpson contest on the back. $5-8.

Frosties cereal box from Kellogg's. U.K. A series of six different Simpsons squirt rings could be found in boxes of this British cereal (*See* Chapter 10 for examples). Box, $5-8.

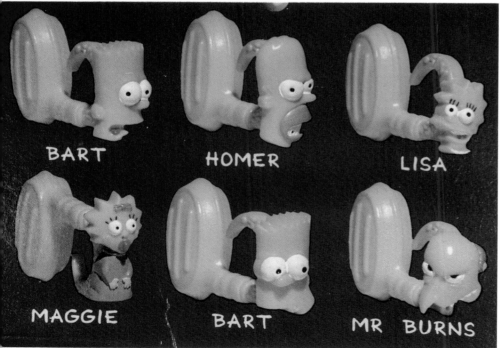

Close-up of the squirt ring set from Frosties box.

Croky double crunch paprika chips, Belgium. One hundred different "Simpsons Caps" were given away in bags of these chips (See Chapter 10 for examples). $5-8.

These 2-liter bottles from Pepsi were part of the *Virtual Simpsons* contest tied in to *The Simpsons'* season premiere in 1997. One lucky viewer could win a replica of the Simpson home by purchasing specially marked 12-packs or 2-liter bottles of Lemon/Lime Slice, Mandarin Orange Slice, Mug Root Beer, Lipton Brisk Iced Tea, and Josta, each of which contained a contest number. Each bottle featured a different family member as well as, in the case of the 12-packs, additional characters from the show. Lisa Slice and Homer Mug bottles, $2-4.

Bart Simpson juice drink packs from Sweetripe Drinks, Canada. Wild Cherry Flavored Apple Drink, Caribbean Punch, Orange A'Licious, Grape Splash. $3-6 each set.

Mandarin Orange Slice 12-pack with Bart and other characters and Josta 12-pack with Bart. Pepsi, $3-6 each. Mandarin Orange Slice 2-liter with Bart, $2-4.

Mug Root Beer 12-pack with Homer and other characters and Lipton Brisk Iced Tea 12-pack with Marge and Maggie and other characters. Pepsi, $3-6 each.

An Australian company (Razorback) produced this can of Springfield's favorite beverage until 20th Century Fox found out about it. Duff: It's Simpsons for beer, mate. $25-40.

Butterfinger Bart banks from Nestle. These plastic banks came filled with mini-Butterfinger bars. Both banks in original packaging, $10-15, separately, $5-8.

Butterfinger Bart bank from Nestle. This metal bank features a hapless Homer about to walk the plank as Blinky awaits. $8-12.

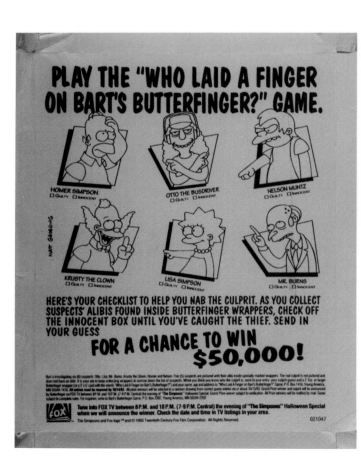

Wrapper for 6-pack of Butterfingers. Nestle. To solve the mystery of who laid a finger on Bart's Butterfinger, one narrowed down the list of six suspects by collecting Butterfinger wrappers. After collecting five different alibis, you sent in the name of the guilty party for a chance to win $50,000. The winner's name was broadcast during *The Simpsons'* 1993 Halloween Special. $3-6.

Inside cardboard from Butterfinger 6-pack. See above.

Bart with Santa's Little Helper and Lisa candy containers. Topps, U.K. $5-8 each.

This set of Simpsons candy filled containers from Topps was available in the U.K.

Homer and Marge/Maggie candy containers from Topps, U.K. $5-8 each.

Chupa Chups "Fantasy Ball" strawberry lollipops with bubble gum centers. Display with pops, $15-20.

Chupa Chups candy and windball, U.K. Talk about value for money, with this set you got a windball toy, a candy whistle, and a Bart pencil topper. $5-8.

Bart bubble gum, nuggets, and tube style from Amurol. $3-5 each.

Bart gumball machine, Lisa and Maggie gumball machine. Jolly Good. $5-8 each.

"A Family For The 90s" collectible plate. This was the first in a series of collector's plates produced by The Franklin Mint. Don't eat off them, though. Mmmmm, toxic. $25-$40.

"Caroling With The Simpsons" collectible plate. Franklin Mint. $25-$40.

"Family Therapy" collectible plate. Franklin Mint. $25-$40.

"Lisa And Her Sax" collectible plate. Franklin Mint. $25-$40.

"Maggie And The Bears" collectible plate. Franklin Mint. $25-$40.

"Three-Eyed Fish" collectible plate. Franklin Mint. $25-$40. The Franklin Mint followed this series of plates with an additional one, "Surfin' Bart" (not pictured here).

Bart cookie jar from
Treasure Chest. $40-$60.

Homer cookie jar.
Treasure Chest. $40-$60.

Bart and Lisa salt and pepper set. Treasure Chest. $25-30.

Homer and Marge salt and pepper set from Treasure Chest.
$35-40.

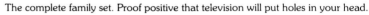

The complete family set. Proof positive that television will put holes in your head.

Chapter Four: Bart's Bedroom

(Board/Video Games, Toys, Objets d' Bart)

The Simpsons Don't Have A Cow
dice game from Milton Bradley.
$10-$15

Don't Have A Cow
board and pieces.

Die Simpsons Mach Dir Keinen Fleck Ins Hemd! dice game from Milton Bradley, Germany. Not an undiscovered Kurt Weill tune, we've been told that the name of this German version of the "Don't Have A Cow" game translates as "Don't Get A Speck On Your Shirt!" $20-25.

The Simpsons Mystery Of Life game from Cardinal. $8-12.

Mystery Of Life board and pieces.

Die Simpsons: Die Geheimnisse Des Lebens game from KidFun, Germany. Identical to the *Mystery Of Life* game, although for some reason the Burping Contest has been mysteriously excised. $20-25.

The Simpsons Board Game from Paul Lamond, U.K. $20-25.

Simpsons Board Game board and pieces.

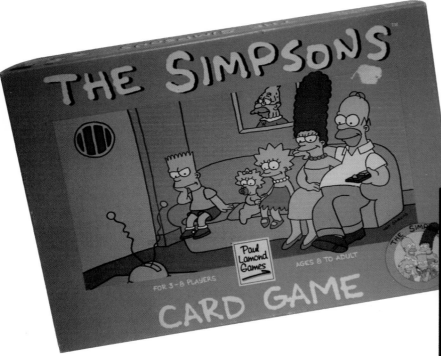

The Simpsons Card Game from Paul Lamond, U.K. $15-20.

Bart Simpson Kartenspiel from Altenburg Stralsunder, Germany. $12-15.

The Simpsons 3-D Checkers set. Manufacturer unknown. $20-25.

The Simpsons 3-D Chess set.
Manufacturer unknown. $30-35.

Chess board and pieces.

Los Simpson card game from
Fournier, Spain. $8-10.

Simpsons domino game from Central Hobby, Japan. $10-15.

Hoopla ring toss game from
Charbens, U.K. $20-25.

Bart Vs. The Space Mutants video game from Nintendo, also available for Genesis and Game Gear. *Bart Vs. The World* by Nintendo, also available for Genesis and Game Gear. The Simpsons video games made clever and original use of many of the show's characters and situations. You can change Bart into Bartman, take a ride down Mt. Splashmore, or make prank phone calls to Moe's. *Krusty's Fun House* (see below), however, is an adaption of a pre-existing U.K. game called *Rat Trap*. $25-30 each.

Bartman Meets Radioactive Man from Nintendo, also available for Genesis and Game Gear. Most of these games came packaged with a free poster of the game box art. $25-30 each.

Bart's Nightmare for Super Nintendo, also available for Genesis. *Krusty's Super Fun House* for Super Nintendo, also available for Genesis, and available as *Krusty's Fun House* for Nintendo, Game Boy, and Game Gear. $25-30 each.

Virtual Bart for Super Nintendo, also available for Genesis. Other video games not pictured: Bart Simpson's Escape From Camp Deadly, Bart Vs. The Juggernauts, Bart And The Beanstalk, and Itchy and Scratchy Golf for Game Boy. Also, The Itchy and Scratchy Game for Super Nintendo, Genesis, and Game Gear. $25-30 each.

Remote control skateboard Bart from Mattel. $25-30.

Bart Simpson skateboard (aka Vehicle Of Destruction) from Sport Fun. $45-50.

Bart skateboard, reverse.

Simpson Car "Elettrica" from Re El Toys, Italy. Battery operated car with directional control pad. Here's a toy that's sure to frighten those law-abiding kids next door. Take turns seeing who can drive it up to the garage door the fastest. With family sticker. $30-40.

Simpsons Walk-A-Long cassette player from JPI. Enjoy your favorite simp-sonic sounds as Bart and Lisa argue. $10-$15.

Bart Simpson phone from Columbia Tel-Com. $15-20

What were they thinking? A spiky-headed demon phone whose eyes light up bright red when it rings? Just where does this hot line go to? Bart's back opens up for push button convenience.

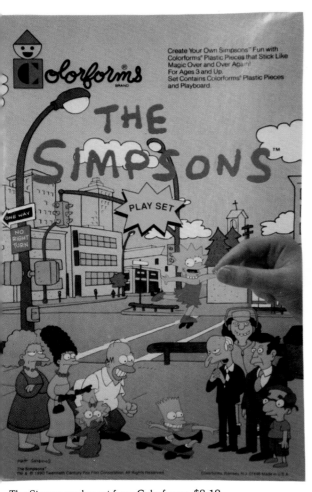

The Simpsons play set from Colorforms. $8-12.

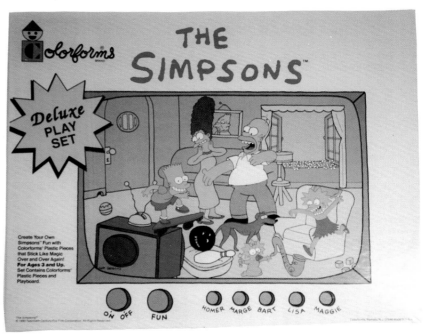

The Simpsons Deluxe play set from Colorforms. $10-15.

The Simpsons Stick N
Lift set from Paul
Lamond, U.K. $8-12.

Easy Paint set #1 (Cool Man and The Simpsons
Family) from Pic, U.K. $10-15.

Easy Paint set #2 (Rain Dance and Bed Time) from Pic, U.K. $10-15.

Homer Simpson inflatable bopper from Helm Toy. $8-12.

Plaster moulding set from Peter Pan, U.K. $10-15.

Bart Simpson bop bag. Helm Toy. $10-15.

Bartman bop bag. Helm Toy. $10-15.

Bart Simpson bubble pipe from Ja-Ru. The budget-priced line of Ja-Ru toys were available through Woolworth's. $5-8.

Bart Simpson sliding puzzles from Ja-Ru. $5-8.

Marge Simpson "Time and Money" set. Ja-Ru. $5-8.

Lisa Simpson double stamp set. Ja-Ru. $5-8.

Bart Simpson target game. Ja-Ru. $5-8.

Homer Simpson target game. Ja-Ru. $5-8.

Simpsons pinball game.
Ja-Ru. $5-8.

Bart Simpson paddle ball. Ja-Ru. $5-8.

Punch balls from Blue Bird.
$2-5.

Bart Simpson yo-yo from
Spectra Star. $5-8.

Bart Simpson bow biters from Brookside. $3-6.

Rad Rollers from Spectra Star. These two sets are different
with the exception of two marbles in common. $5-8.

Bart Simpson stretch belt from Pyramid. $5-8.

Bart Simpson flashlight from Happiness Express. $5-8.

100-piece puzzles from Milton Bradley. $3-6.

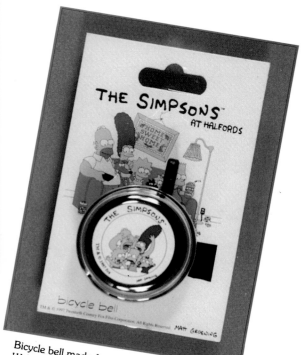

Bicycle bell made for Halfords stores by Weldtite, U.K. $8-12.

100-piece puzzle. Milton Bradley. $3-6.

Homer and Marge ceramic magnets. $3-6.

Simpsons word magnets from Fridge Fun, $6-10. Bart Simpson sliding puzzle from Jotastar, U.K. $5-8.

Simpsons Bio-Genetic Reconstruction Kits, Volumes 1 and 2 from Caryco Magnets. Splice the genes of The Simpsons and create advanced life forms like the terrifying "Homarge." The Future is D'oh! $15-20.

This TV-shaped viewing toy from Germany is the only kind of Simpsons related viewer I've found. By pressing a lever on the side, you can view scenes from the episode, "The Crepes Of Wrath." Plastiskop. $6-$10.

Coca-Cola/Sprite magnets from Coca-Cola. $3-6 each.

Bart Simpson "Who The Hell Are You?" cap from Universal. $5-8.

Homer Simpson "All American Dad" cap from Universal. $5-8.

"Simpsons In The Dark" caps from Head Start. Barney, Krusty, and Lisa. $8-12.

"Simpsons In The Dark" caps. Head Start. Bart and Homer. $8-12.

"Simpsons In The Dark" caps. Head Start. Bart and Homer. $8-12.

Bartman mask from Cowan, de Groot, U.K. $7-10. Marge mask from Ben Cooper. $5-8.

Sheva brought this Bart Simpson mask all the way back from the Rock of Gibraltar for me. And you wondered why she rated a Dedication? From Josman, Spain. $8-12.

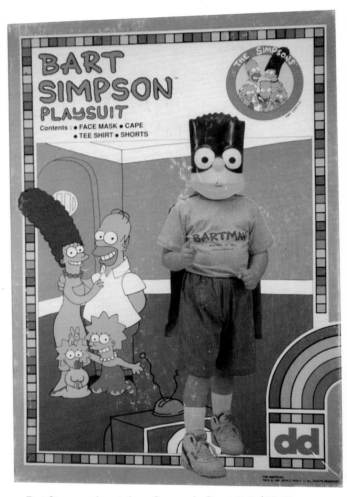

Bart Simpson playsuit from Cowan, de Groot, U.K. $10-15.

Flat Halloween masks from Norben, Canada. $4-8 each.

Vacuform Halloween masks. Norben, Canada. $4-8 each.

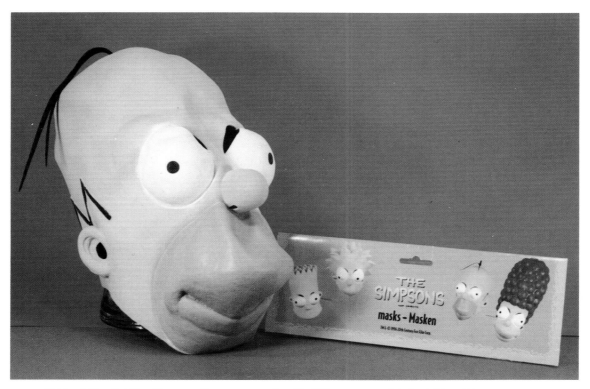

Yabba dabba d'oh! Looking more like a caveman than Fred Flintstone ever did, this full head Homer mask from A La Carte does a fine job of reproducing the day-old beard that's an indispensable part of any animated patriarch. (Why Yogi Bear had it is yet another of the ancient cartoon mysteries.) The complete set, released in 1996, included Bart, Lisa, Homer, and Marge. Germany. $30-40.

Full head Radioactive Man mask. One year later, Bartman and Radioactive Man (complete with lightning bolt!) were added to the collection. A La Carte, Germany. $30-40.

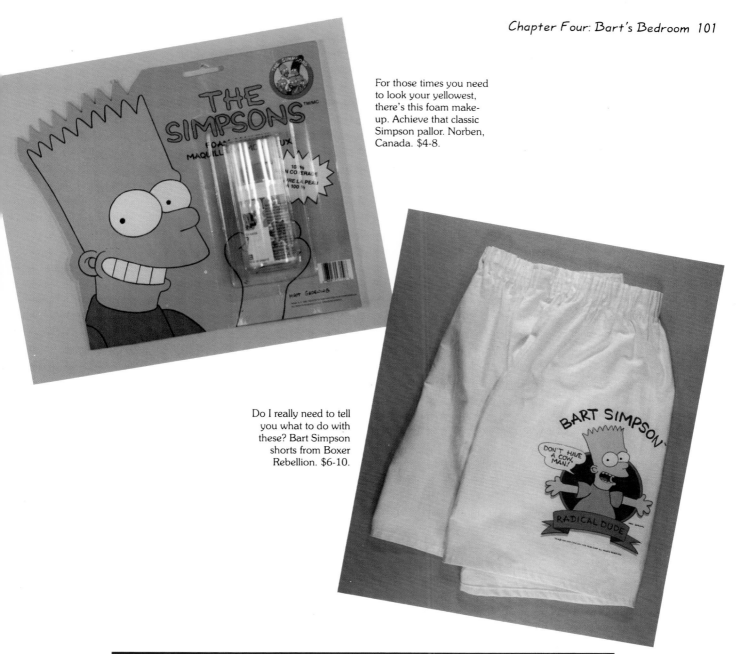

For those times you need to look your yellowest, there's this foam make-up. Achieve that classic Simpson pallor. Norben, Canada. $4-8.

Do I really need to tell you what to do with these? Bart Simpson shorts from Boxer Rebellion. $6-10.

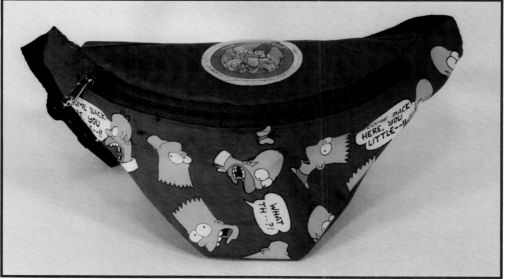

Purple belt-bag from Imaginings 3. $6-10.

Bart and Lisa travel bag.
Imaginings 3. $12-16.

Bart gloves from the U.K. $8-12.

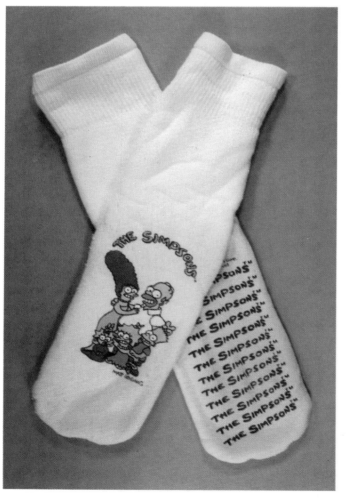

Socks, manufacturer unknown. $5-8.
Courtesy of Sheva Golkow.

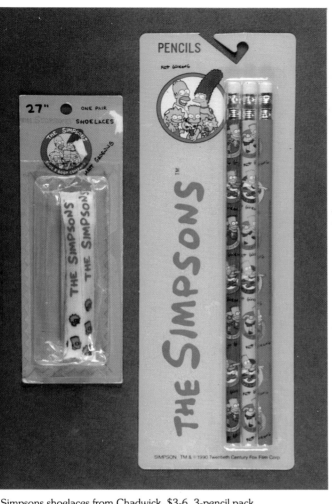

Lampshade, U.K. $8-12.

Simpsons shoelaces from Chadwick. $3-6. 3-pencil pack
from Legends. $3-6.

Pillow case from Bibb.
$3-5.

Simpsons comforter from Bibb. $15-20.

Simpsons wallpaper, U.K. $10-15.

Kid's room signs from H&L. $3-6 each.

Kid's room signs. H&L. $3-6 each.

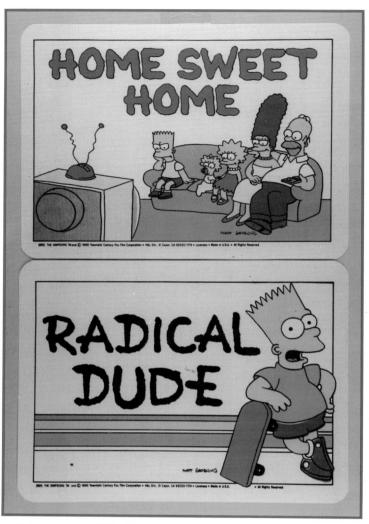

Kid's room signs. H&L. $3-6 each.

Kid's room signs. H&L. $3-6 each.

Suction cup signs. H&L. $2-4.

Bart bumper stickers from NJ Croce Co. $3-6.

Bart picture frame from Tropico, France. $15-18.

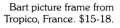

Bart license plate frame from NJ Croce Co. Guaranteed to cut down on road rage. $4-6.

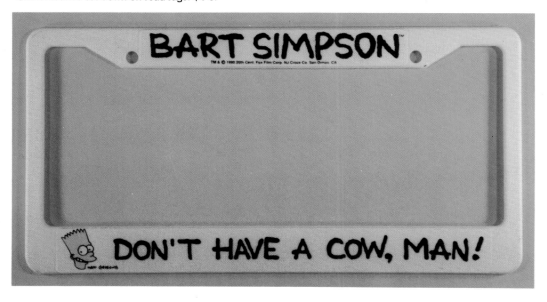

Bart Simpson frisbee, promo for Dash detergent, U.K. $5-8.

Bart Simpson metal bank from Tropico, France. $8-12.

Bart Simpson key ring from Street Kids. This key ring was also available with different colored shirts on Bart. $3-6.

Cloisonne key rings from Gift Creations. Based on Gift's popular cloisonne pins. $3-6 each.

Family key ring, rubber. $3-6. Bart key ring from Downpace, U.K. $5-8.
Personalized key ring from U.K. $5-8.

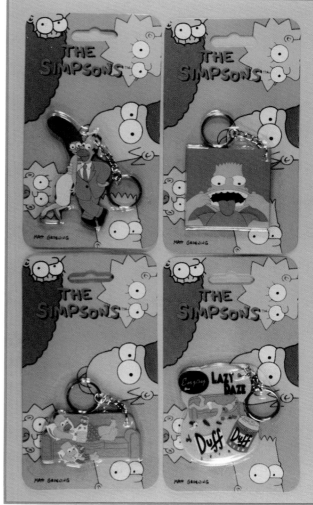

Four vinyl key rings from Vivid Imaginations, U.K. These British
key rings were also available as vinyl magnets. $3-5 each.

Two Bart key rings. Vivid
Imaginations, U.K. $3-5 each.

Invitation to the underpants.
Framed poster from Western. $3-6.

Die Simpsons super-poster set from Xenos, Germany. $8-12.

Die Simpsons super-poster set
from Xenos, Germany. $8-12.

Coloring sheets from Editorial Publica, Portugal. Sets #2 (*Em Casa*) and #3 (*No Desporto*), $5-7 each.

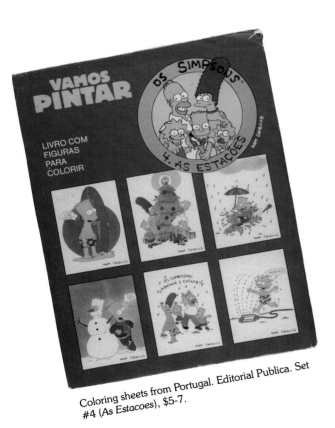

Coloring sheets from Portugal. Editorial Publica. Set #4 (*As Estacoes*), $5-7.

The Simpsons Christmas stocking from Copywrite, U.K. What kid wouldn't love school supplies for Christmas? Maybe this belongs in Lisa's section... $5-$8.

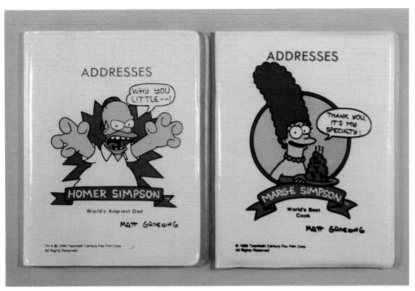

Homer and Marge address books. Legends. $3-6.

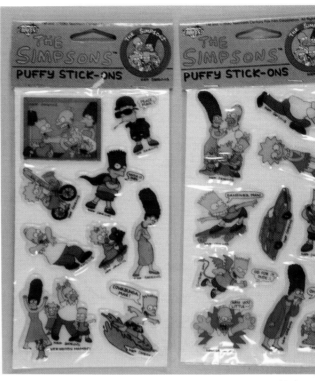

Puffy stick-ons from Diamond. Two different sets. $3-6.

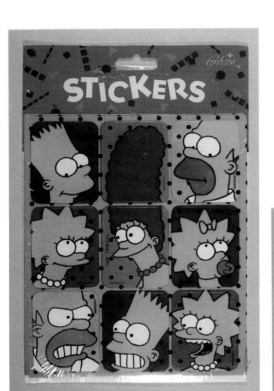

Stickers from Gibson. I especially like the fact that it takes two stickers to accommodate both Marge *and* her hair. $2-4.

Church's Chicken promo chalks. $2-4.

Rubber stamps from Rubber Stampede. Rubber Stampede produced an entire line of quality Simpsons stamps totaling fourteen or more. $8-12.

Air fresheners from Medo. $3-6.

Phone card from Frontier. Bart in phone booth. $10-15.

Phone card from Frontier. Homer dials 911. $10-15.

Phone card from Frontier. Marge's ringing hair. $10-15.

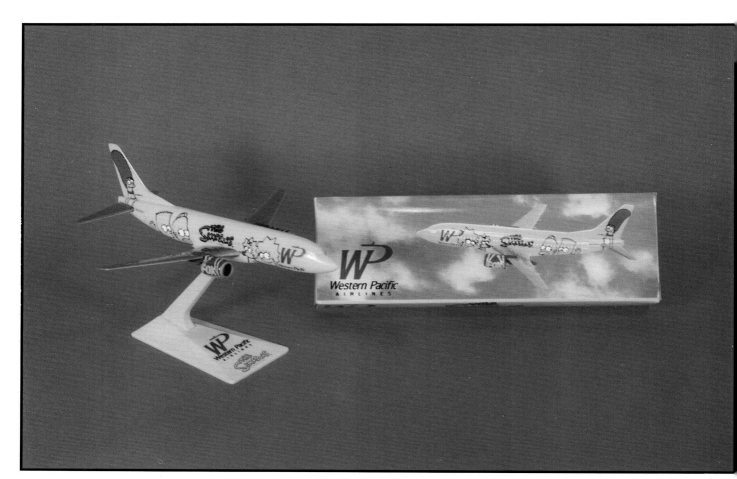

Plastic replica of the actual Western Pacific Simpsons plane. With custom stand. $25-30.

Chapter Five: Lisa's Bedroom

(Clocks/Watches, School Supplies, Hair Accessories)

Simpsons wall clock from JPI. $20-25.

Bart Simpson mini clock from Nelsonic. $25-30.

Bart Simpson FM clock radio with Alarm from JPI. $20-25.

Bart Simpson talking alarm clock from
Wesco, U.K. $30-35.

Keep your Mona Lisa. Take back your Sistine Chapel. This Simpsons talking radio alarm clock from Wesco redefines the meaning of the word masterpiece. With a light-up TV, Duff beer cans that double as a volume dial, a lamp radio tuner, and digital clock, this homey (or Homey) tableau dazzles the eye and irritates the ear with real Simpson voices. *Simpsons* collectibles reach a sort of almost mystical apotheosis with this frightening gadget. U.K., $40-50.

Above: Bart Simpson watch, blue band with name, from Nelsonic. Dancing family watch, blue band. Nelsonic. $8-12.
Below: Itchy and Scratchy Show watches from Big Time. Filmstrip watch and Hot dog vendor Itchy watch with green band. True to the spirit of the cartoon, Scratchy's decapitated head actually floats inside the watch! $10-15.

Above: Bart Simpson watch, blue band, from Nelsonic. Bartman watch, black band. Nelsonic. $8-12.
Below: Itchy and Scratchy Show watches. Big Time. Barber Itchy watch with black band and Acid cocktail watch with blue band. It's always time for animated cruelty! $10-15.

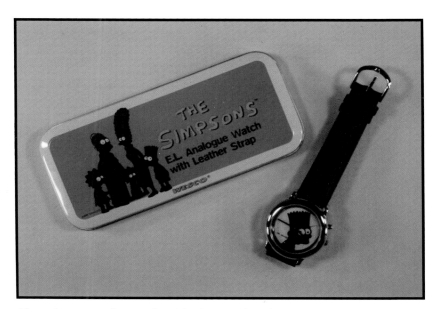

Electro-luminescent Bart watch with leather strap from Wesco, U.K. Press a button and the watchface lights up light blue. A Homer model was also available. $25-35.

Bartman watch, black band with name. Nelsonic. $8-12.

Giant hanging watch from Zeon, U.K. $20-25.

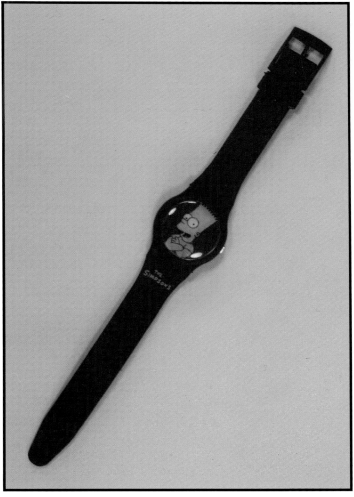

Bart watch from Subway. The cover for this digital watch features a "flickering" Bart that changes from introvert to extrovert. $3-5.

Bart Simpson diary set from Legends. $8-12.

Nope, it's not the Spice Girls. Bart erasers from Street Kids. $3-5.

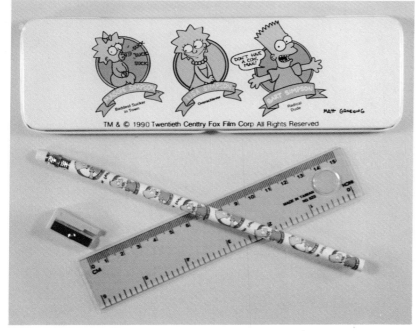

Metal pencil case with pencil, ruler, and sharpener from Legends. $4-8.

Maggie note pad from Legends. $3-6.

Simpsons school kit from Imaginings 3. $7-10.

Two different lunch thermoses from Thermos. There were also other variations produced. $5-8 each.

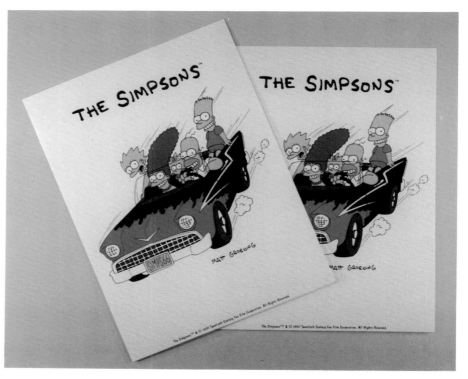

Paper folders from Class Acts. $1-3.

Bart Simpson metal pencil cases from Mitsubishi, Japan. These metal cases from Japan, which refer to Bart as the "Bad Boy Of Springfield," are beautifully detailed. $12-16.

Detail from pink metal pencil case, Japan.

Detail from green metal pencil case, Japan.

Bart Simpson metal pencil case from Copywrite, U.K. $6-10. Simpsons metal pencil case from Mitsubishi, Japan. $12-16.

Detail from Simpsons metal pencil case, Japan.

Metal pencil case from Copywrite, U.K. $8-12. Metal pencil case from Hungry Jack's restaurant promotion, Australia. $8-12.

Simpsons plastic lunch box from Thermos. $8-12, $12-15 with thermos.

Bart with surfboard earrings from Toonies, U.K. $7-10.

Lisa hair bands from Wow Wee, decorated with Bart or Lisa. $3-6.

Simpsons valentines, set of thirty-two from Cleo. I choo-choo-choose you! $3-6.

Homer mouse pad from Office Gear. You can proudly proclaim your work ethic to your co-workers with this. $8-12.

Computer screen frame from Screenies. $7-10.

Bart and Lisa pony tail holders. Wow Wee. $3-6.

Bart with slingshot and Family pony tail holders. Wow Wee. $3-6.

Bart and Surfin' Bart hair clips. Wow Wee. $3-6.

Family and Lisa hair clips. Wow Wee. $3-6.

Chapter Six: Living Room

(Cels and Drawings, CDs, Tapes and Videos)

Anyone who collects ephemera dealing with animation is sooner or later going to be faced with whether or not to invest in original art. There's nothing more exciting than actually owning an original piece of artwork, or *production cel*, from a favorite episode. Usually framed with an authentic background, the price of a cel can vary depending on the number of characters in the picture and the popularity of the characters. Any reputable animation art dealer can give you more information about original art and will probably be happy to send you some xeroxed examples of what's available.

In addition to original production cels, however, there are also some related kinds of art available:

Production drawings: These are rough pencil sketches by the animators and are generally much more affordable than cels. Expect to spend something in the vicinity of $40-70.

Original Cel without background: Uncommon, but still much less expensive than an original framed cel. The lack of an authentic background allows these to go for around $50-80.

Authorized Sericels: From time to time, limited edition cels, or *sericels*, are produced. The price of these can vary widely, generally depending on the limitation. Simpsons sericels have been made available for as little as $125 or as much as $2,000. Ask an animation dealer for more information about what's currently available.

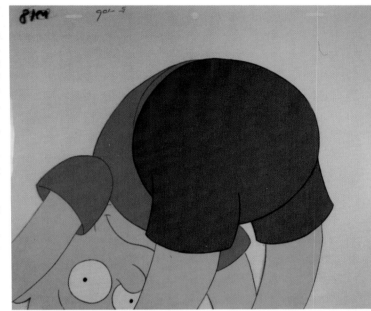

Bart strikes a characteristic pose. Loose cel without background. $50-60.

Production drawing of Homer, matted. $40-50.

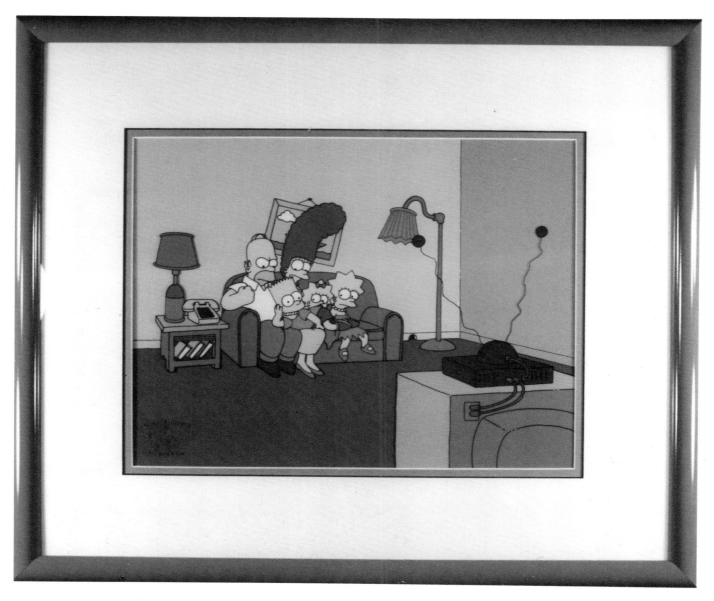

"Bart-O-Lounger" sericel released by Fox to celebrate *The Simpsons*' 100th episode. $100-$120.

Right: *The Simpsons Sing The Blues* on Geffen. The first Simpsons album matched the characters up with guest stars like B.B. King, Joe Walsh, Buster Poindexter, D.J. Jazzy Jeff, and Dr. John. Highlights include Homer's *Born Under A Bad Sign* and Smithers and Mr. Burns' *Look At All Those Idiots.* CD $14-18, cassette $8-12.

Opposite page:
Bottom right: Much trickier to find is the album's vinyl version, as that format was on the way out at the time and most copies were promos intended for radio stations (as the magic marker on this copy attests). $12-16.

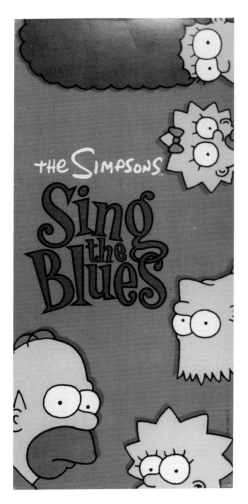

Original CD box for *The Simpsons Sing The Blues*. $6-10.

Back of display box with punch-out Bart. Geffen.

Deep, Deep Trouble 7-inch vinyl single from Geffen, U.K. $7-10. *Do The Bartman* promo CD from Geffen. Inside the gatefold...

...you'll find a CD with six different mixes of *Do The Bartman* in a sleeve with lyrics and a special cartoon flip book that lets you *see* Bart dance and dry his hair. $10-15.

Do The Bartman, limited edition shaped picture disc. Geffen, U.K. $10-15.

Deep, Deep Trouble, limited edition shaped picture disc. Geffen, U.K. $10-15.

Theme From The Simpsons sheet music from Warner Bros. and *Do The Bartman* from Hal Leonard. Contrary to popular belief, this sheet music proves that the *Simpsons* theme actually has lyrics. They go like this: "The Simp-sons!" $8-12.

Songs In The Key Of Springfield from Rhino Records. Rather than offer all-new material this time, the second Simpsons release shone the spotlight on the witty contributions of the versatile Alf Clausen. Guest stars galore and too many classics to count, including *Who Needs The Kwik-E-Mart?*, *See My Vest*, and umpteen versions of the show's theme song. Both the CD and cassette were also available in special "blister packs" which allowed them to be more easily stocked in the store's children's section. CD $14-18, cassette $8-12. *God Bless The Child* promo CD from *Sings The Blues* album. Geffen. $5-8.

The Simpsons Christmas Special from Fox Video. This was the only Simpsons video available in U.S. stores until the release of first season episodes in 1997. $7-10.

The Best Of The Simpsons video set. Fox Video. At long last, years after episodes had been available for purchase in Europe, Fox began to make uncut versions of *Simpsons* episodes available on VHS. Volume One: *There's No Disgrace Like Home* and *Life On The Fast Lane*. Volume Two: *Bart The General* and *Moaning Lisa*. Volume Three: *The Crepes Of Wrath* and *Krusty Gets Busted*. $7-10 each, $18-25 for the boxed set.

Audio cassettes of episodes of *Die Simpsons* from Karussell, Germany. $8-12.

Books seem to run a very distant second to television in the Simpson household. In one episode, Homer did his bit for paper recycling by rounding up all the books in the house and dumping them in a trash can. Until someone invents the deep-fried novel, the only books you're likely to find there would probably be in Lisa's room, not counting the vast archive of Radioactive Man comics in Bart's room, of course, or the occasional non-threatening romance novel on Marge's bedtable.

The first Simpsons book to find its way into print was *Greetings From The Simpsons* (HarperPerennial), a post-

La Navidad De Los Simpson from Ediciones B. Hardback, Spain. $10-15.

card book. Working with a talented staff under Groening's supervision, HarperPerennial produced a steady stream of kid's books throughout the '90s .In 1991, the same team was responsible for *Simpsons Illustrated*, an official quarterly magazine chock full of interviews, reader's drawings and pull-out newspaper inserts like the "Springfield Shopper." They also mark the first appearance of The Simpsons in comic book format. Lasting for ten issues (one of which was produced entirely in 3-D!), copies of *Simpsons Illustrated* are difficult to find today. A smaller edition of the magazine was also produced for promotional purposes.

The comic book sections of the magazine had been so successful that in early 1993, *Simpsons Comics and Stories* #1 appeared. Intended to test the waters for a possible series of Simpson comics, it did well enough to launch the Bongo Comics Group later that year. Named after one of the characters in Groening's *Life In Hell* strip, Bongo made a splash with four different titles: *Simpsons Comics*, *Bartman*, *Itchy and Scratchy Comics*, and *Radioactive Man*. The idea behind *Radioactive Man* was particularly clever. Conceived as a limited 6-issue series, each issue was numbered as if it had come from a different year in his long and checkered career. This format allowed the artists and writers to parody the whole spectrum of the history of comics, from the Golden Age to present-day "Dark Knight" style angst. Most recently, Radioactive Man reappeared in an 80-page

collection that poked affectionate fun at the "80 Page Giants" that D.C. Comics used to produce during the Silver Age.

The first four premiere issues each came with a pull-out poster which, when combined with the other three, created a large mural featuring all the characters. A smaller version of this was also produced as a single poster for comics retailers. The first four were also collected in an exclusive hardback, *Bongo Comics Extravaganza*, limited to 1,000 copies and sent to retailers. Although most of their titles were conceived as a limited series, *Simpsons Comics* continues to be published on a regular basis and collected periodically in trade paperback format. An occasional mini-series featuring other characters, like Lisa and Krusty The Clown, appears from time-to-time. The *Bartman* and *Radioactive Man* titles have also inspired cards in the Skybox Simpsons Cards sets (see Trading Cards).

A Bongo Checklist

Simpsons Comics #1-32. Ongoing bi-monthly title.
Bartman #1-6. Limited series.
Itchy and Scratchy Comics #1-3. Limited series.
Itchy and Scratchy Holiday Hi-Jinx Special #1. One-shot.
Radioactive Man #1-6 (or #1, #88, #216, #412, #679, and #1000). Limited series.
Radioactive Man 80-page Colossal #1. One-Shot.
Krusty Comics #1-3. Limited series.
Bart Simpson's Treehouse Of Horror #1-3. Published once a year.
Lisa Comics #1. One-shot.

Greetings From The Simpsons, a postcard book from HarperPerennial, 1990. $4-8.

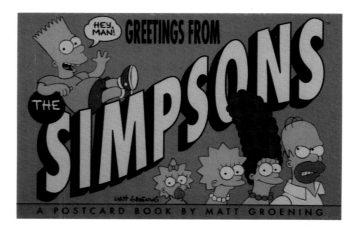

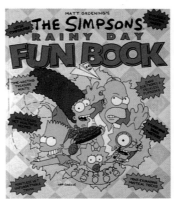 

The Simpsons Xmas Book from HarperPerennial, 1990. Hardback, $8-12, softback, $5-8. *Le Livre De Noel Des Simpson* from Albin Michel, France. Hardback. $10-15.

The Simpsons Rainy Day Fun Book. HarperPerennial softcover, 1991. *Los Simpson Libro De Juegos para los Dias de Lluvia.* Ediciones B hardback. Spain. $10-15 each.

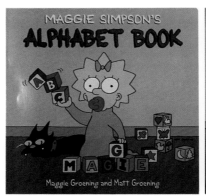 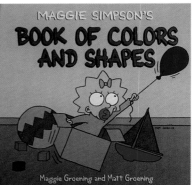

Maggie Simpson's Alphabet Book and *Book Of Colors And Shapes.* HarperPerennial, 1991. This series of children's books was written by Maggie Groening along with her brother Matt. $4-7 each.

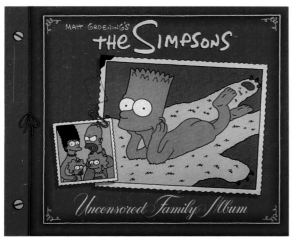

The Simpsons Uncensored Family Album. HarperPerennial, 1991. This collection of family photos and keepsakes includes a definitive family tree which reveals that one of the Simpsons' distant relations is one Charles Montgomery Burns. $10-15.

Maggie Simpson's Counting Book and *Book Of Animals.* HarperPerennial, 1991. The four Maggie Simpson books are now out-of-print. $4-7 each.

The Simpsons Ultra-Jumbo Rain-Or-Shine Fun Book. HarperPerennial softcover, 1993. This double-size volume contained both the *Fun In The Sun* book (not pictured) and the *Rainy Day Fun Book. Los Simpson Juegos y Pasatiempos para Dias del Sol.* Ediciones B hardback. Spain. $10-15 each.

Making Faces With The Simpsons, A Book Of Masks.
HarperPerennial, 1992. $7-10.

Cartooning With The Simpsons. HarperPerennial softcover, 1993.
Aprende a Dibujar con Los Simpson. Ediciones B hardback. Spain.
$10-15 each.

Bart Simpson's Guide To Life. HarperPerennial hardback,
1993. Bart Simpson's Guia para la Vida from Ediciones B.
Softcover, Spain. $10-15.

Simpsons Comics Extravaganza (Simpsons Comics 1-4) and
Simpsons Comics Spectacular (Simpsons Comics 6-9) from
HarperPerennial. $8-12.

The Simpsons: A Complete Guide To Our Favorite Family.
HarperPerennial softcover, 1997. This long awaited guide to every
episode of The Simpsons flew off the shelves when it arrived in late 1997.
Only the first printing features all family members on the spine; all later
printings show only Bart and Homer. $15-18. I Can't Believe It's An
Unofficial Simpsons Guide.Virgin Books, U.K. This unauthorized guide to
the show, which beat the official one to store shelves by only a few
months, is also filled with facts and trivia. There's also a guide to
Simpsons comics as an appendix. $8-12.

Bartman:The Best Of The Best (Bartman 1-3 and When Bongos
Collide trilogy) and Simpsons Comics Simps-O-Rama (Simpsons
Comics 11-14). HarperPerennial. $8-12.

Simpsons Comics Strike Back! (*Simpsons Comics* 15-18) and
Simpsons Comics Wing Ding (*Simpsons Comics* 19-23).
HarperPerennial. $8-12.

The Simpsons 1991 Fun Calendar from Random
House. *Simpsons* calendars were produced every
year from 1991 to 1995. $5-8.

*Bongo Comics
Group Spectacular*,
one of a limited
edition of 1,000
copies. This special
hardback edition of
the first four Bongo
comics was sent to
comics retailers and
occasionally given
away as a contest
prize. The only
Simpsons book ever
to be granted the
dignity of a dust
jacket. $40-60.

The Simpsons 1994 Fun Calendar. How many other
calendars let you know when to celebrate the birthdays
of Ernie Kovacs, Charles Addams, Tex Avery, Vivian
Stanshall, Charles Mingus, Sid Vicious, Maurice Sendak,
Raymond Chandler, Marcel Duchamp, Walt Kelly, Elvis
Costello, Peter Cook, and Philip K. Dick? Precious few,
I'll wager. Random House. $5-8.

Simpson Mania from Publications International.
Hardback, $5-8. Spiral-bound, $3-6. *The Simpsons A
to Z.* Publications International, $3-6.

Simpsons Illustrated, Issue #1, Spring 1991. $7-10.
Smaller promo version, $3-5.

Simpsons Illustrated, Issue #1, Spring 1991 and Issue #2, Summer 1991 from Welsh Publishing. #1, $7-10. #2, $5-8.

Simpsons Illustrated, Issue #3, Fall 1991 and Issue #4, Winter 1992. Welsh Publishing. $5-8 each.

Simpsons Illustrated, Issue #5, Spring 1992 and Issue #6, Summer 1992. Welsh Publishing. $5-8 each.

Simpsons Illustrated, Issue #7, Fall 1992 and 1992 3-D Annual. Welsh Publishing. This 3-D annual is a must: the entire issue, comics, ads and all, is in 3-D and comes with special "Simps-O-Vision" glasses. $5-8.

Simpsons Illustrated, Issue #8, Winter 1993 and Issue #9, Summer 1993. Welsh Publishing. $5-8. This would be the last issue of *SI* to appear, although Welsh would also bring out the first and only issue of *Simpsons Comics and Stories,* the prelude to the creation of the Bongo Comics Group.

Bart Simpson's Joke Book. This collection of gags and vignettes appeared as a supplement to *Hero Illustrated* #24, June 1995. $3-6. *Simpsons Comics and Stories* #1 from Welsh Publishing, 1993. This one-shot was meant as a test to gauge the interest in a continuing series of Simpsons comics. It came polybagged with a Bartman and Radioactive Man poster. $5-8.

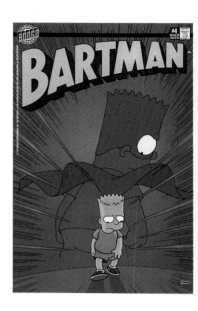

The Dawn Of The Bongo Age Of Comics. A selection of Bongo comics, including some of the *Simpsons Comics* back covers that featured supporting characters.

Bartman #4. Like the TV show, the various Simpsons comic titles were chock full of homages and in-jokes. This dramatic cover pays tribute to the classic cover of *The Amazing Spider-Man #50* from 1967. (They weren't the first, though: *Howard The Duck* actually beat them to it in the late 1970s.)

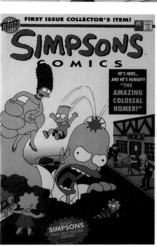

Krusty Comics #1 and *Lisa Comics #1*. Bongo. *Lisa Comics* was a one-shot. *Krusty* is of particular interest, too, as it's the only official comic to significantly alter the characters' "studio" look. *Krusty*, $3-6. *Lisa*, $3-6.

The first four #1 issues from Bongo each came with a special pull-out poster that fit with the other three to make one colossal mural. (A smaller version also appeared as a promotional poster for the "When Bongos Collide!" crossover.) Comics fans will also recognize an homage to *Fantastic Four #1* on the cover of *Simpsons Comics #1*. The cover of *Radioactive Man #1* actually glows in the dark! *Simpsons Comics #1*, $5-8. *Radioactive Man #1*, $5-8.

Bartman and Radioactive Man #1 mini-comic available with *Hero Illustrated #12*. Reprints "Lo, There Shall Be A Bartman!" from *Simpsons Comics And Stories*. $3-6. *Itchy and Scratchy Holiday Hi-Jinx Special #1* from Bongo, $3-6.

Bartman #1 and *Itchy and Scratchy Comics #1* from Bongo Comics Group. Both come with pull-out posters. The cover of *Bartman #1* is actually enhanced with the same kind of silver ink Bartman is about to fall into. *Bartman #1*, $5-8. *Itchy and Scratchy Comics #1*, $5-8.

Bart Simpson's Treehouse of Horror #1 and *80 Page Colossal Radioactive Man* #1. Bongo. *Treehouse Of Horror* borrowed the format of *The Simpsons'* annual Halloween special, while the *80 Page Radioactive Man* special poked affectionate fun at the "80-Page Giant" collections of Comics' Silver Age. *Treehouse,* $3-6. *80 Page RM,* $4-7.

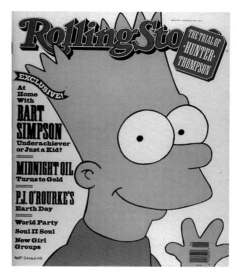

Rolling Stone, #581, June 28th, 1990. $7-10.

One of a limited edition of 500 specially signed copies of *Bart Simpson's Treehouse Of Horror* #1. Signed on October 25th, 1995, at Los Angeles' Golden Apple Comics, this one's a special favorite as it features the signatures of not only Matt Groening and artist Bill Morrison, but those of the creators of two of the 1990s most memorable comic heroes, *Starman's* James Robinson and *Madman's* Mike Allred who both lent their talents to this issue. $25-35.

 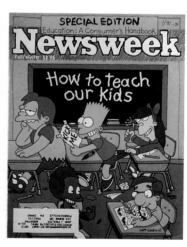

Kids' Stuff comic catalog #1, April 1997. $1-3. *Newsweek* Special Issue, Fall/Winter 1990. $3-5.

Simpsons Comics #1, March '97 and #2, April '97 from Titan Books, U.K. These large format versions of *Simpsons Comics* contain the same stories as their U.S counterparts, along with back-up articles from *Simpsons Illustrated* and new and original letters pages. $8-12.

Cracked, #295, Dec.1994. $3-5. *Time,* Dec. 31, 1990. $3-5.

Here's Good and Evil in a yellow nutshell. *New York*, Feb. 26, 1996. $4-6. *Keyboard*, January 1993. $4-6.

Mad's legendary caricaturist Mort Drucker tries his hand at yet another icon. *Mad*, #299, Dec. 1990. $3-5. *Entertainment Weekly*, June 28/July 5 1991. $3-5.

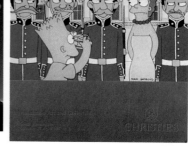

GamePro, November 1991. $4-6. *Mother Jones*, May/June 1991. $4-6.

Hero Illustrated, # 19, January 1995. $4-6. *Christie's* catalog, *Animation Art and Collectibles*, April 1992. $5-8.

Film Score Monthly, March/April 1997. $4-6. *Cards Illustrated*, Sept. 1994. $4-6.

TV Guide, March 17-23, 1990. $6-10. *Disney Adventures*, February 1994. $3-5. *TV Guide* (Canada), March 29-April 4, 1997. $8-12.

Animation Magazine, Oct./Nov. 1995. $4-6. *Overstreet Comic Book Monthly*, Nov. 1993. $4-6.

Hero Illustrated, #5, November 1993. This cover only appeared on the newsstand version of Issue #5. Copies sold through the direct comic book market had a non-Simpsons cover. $5-8. *Advance Comics*, #76, April 1995. $3-5.

Bart Simpson Vs. The Space Mutants poster from *Nintendo Power*, #20, Jan.1991. $3-5.

The Comics Journal, #141, April 1991. *Life In Hell*'s Bongo confronts Bart on this Matt Groening cover. $4-6. *Combo*, #3, April 1995. $4-6.

Previews, October 1993. This issue of *Previews* also came with a large promo card for the first set of Skybox Simpsons Cards bound in. $3-5. *Comic Shop News*, #332, 11/3/93. $2-4.

Krusty's Fun House poster from *Nintendo Power*, #36, May 1992. $3-5.

Hot Dog!, #67, Scholastic Books. $4-6. This Milk Board ad featuring Bart and Lisa appeared in numerous publications (including the inside back cover of the January 17, 1997, issue of *Entertainment Weekly* seen here) and as a bus stop poster in early 1997. Lisa implores Bart to "have a cow." As poster, $3-6.

Comic Shop News Fall Preview, 1995. $2-4. *Rhino Direct* catalog #34 from Rhino Records. $1-3.

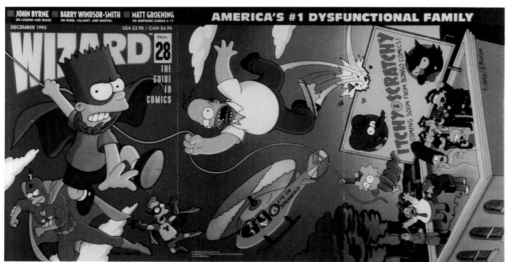

Wizard, #28, December 1993. The cover of this issue of *Wizard* unfolded to reveal an impressive three-part mural. $4-6.

TV Guide produced four different Simpsons "collectors' covers" for their Jan. 3-9, 1998 issue. The four covers fit together to create an extended couch scene. Set, $5-8.

Chapter Eight: Buttons/Pins

6-pack of Simpsons pins from Button-Up. Buttons were also sold separately from a cardboard display (see below). $4-6.

"Fun Has A Name" and Family jumbo pins. Button-Up. $3-6 each.

"Cool Your Jets" and "Aye Carumba!" jumbo pins. Button-Up. $3-6 each.

"Underachiever" and "B. Simpson, Esquire" jumbo pins from Button-Up. $3-6 each.

Bartman jumbo pin. Button-Up. $3-6 each.

Simpsons pins from Avanti. $3-6 each.

Simpsons flatpins. Pinpoint. $2-5 each.

Simpsons flatpins from Pinpoint. $2-5 each.

Simpsons flatpins. Pinpoint. $2-5 each.

Cardboard display for Button-Up pins. $3-6.

Family and Bart pins. $3-6 each. Promo pins from Bongo Comics Group, Homer, Apu and Grampa. $3-6 each.

Cloisonne pins from Gift Creations. Authentic pin should read "Gift Creations, Inc." on the back. If "Nat'l Television Mkt." appears, pin is from Ultra Premium, Canada. If neither name appears, you've got a bootleg. In this picture, the *Bartman*, *Atomic Dad*, and *Go For It* pins are Canadian, while the *Homer and Marge* pin is a bootleg. Strangely, the licensed Canadian *Atomic Dad* pin contains a bootleg-like error, with a "Man Groening" credit on the front. The *Flying Lisa* pin is not from Gift, but a Bongo Comics pin available through comic stores. Gift also created key chain versions of these pins. $3-6 each.

Promo pin from T.G.I. Friday's, $5-8. Promo pin from Butterfinger, $5-8. Promo pins from Ramada Inn, $3-6 each.

Promo pin for Cable Channel 13 in Portland, Oregon. Bart badge, U.K. $3-6.

Unlicensed pins: Anti-war Bart, "Elect The Underachievers In '92" (Bart with Dan Quayle!), "O.J. Or Homer," $3-6 each.

Chapter Nine: Trading Cards/Greeting Cards

Promo poster for the 1990 Topps set of Simpsons cards.

This early set of collectible trading cards from Topps contained eighty-eight cards and twenty-two stickers. Complete set, $8-12.

The Glow-In-The-Dark cards from the first Skybox Simpsons set: Smilin' Joe Fission, Eyeballs, TV, and Shock!

Two promo cards from the first Skybox Simpsons set. Overlay cel card C1 on to Homer card B1 to create a cozy family scene.

The Simpsons Trading Cards, first series from Skybox. 1994. This series is so far superior to the Topps set that comparing them is really unfair. Drawing on both the TV show and the Simpson-related comics produced by the Bongo Comics Group, these cards are loaded with great art, clever character descriptions, and all kinds of limited "chase" cards to track down (see list). A home run by any standard. 10,000 10-box cases were produced. A special Redemption card could be redeemed for an "Art de Bart" card with an original drawing of Bart by Matt Groening. Basic set (Character cards, Itchy & Scratchy cards, Radioactive Man cards), $8-12. Tattoo cards, 10-25 cents each. Wiggle cards, $1-3 each. Glow-in-the-Dark cards, $5-8 each. Cel cards, $7-10 each. Promo cards, $1-3 each. Redemption card, $75-100. Art de Bart card, $300-500.

Cel cards from the first Skybox Simpsons set. Scratchy gets a shave that's a little too close.

Cel cards from the first Skybox Simpsons set. The Simpsons invite the entire town over to watch TV.

The Simpsons card can. Skybox. Featuring the same graphics seen on the Skybox Simpsons Card box and wrappers, this cool looking collectible was available only as a mail-order promotion offered on the back of the card pack. The card set fits inside a red plastic base that sits in the bottom of it. $5-8.

The Simpsons Trading Cards, SkyBox, 1993

Character Cards
S1. Homer Simpson
S2. Marge Simpson
S3. Bart Simpson
S4. Lisa Simpson
S5. Maggie Simpson
S6. Chief Wiggum
S7. Kent Brockman
S8. Lenny
S9. Sideshow Bob
S10. Apu Nahasapeemapetilon
S11. Tattoo Annie
S12. Mrs. Krabappel
S13. Mr. Largo
S14. Janey Powell
S15. Nelson Muntz
S16. Jimbo Jones
S17. Bumblebee Man
S18. Milhouse Van Houten
S19. Sideshow Mel
S20. Krusty The Clown
S21. Lurleen Lumpkin
S22. Groundskeeper Willie
S23. Rabbi Krustofski
S24. Princess Kashmir
S25. Jasper
S26. Patty & Selma
S27. Grampa Simpson
S28. Smilin' Joe Fission
S29. Capital City Goofball
S30. Snowball II
S31. Bill & Marty
S32. Capt. Lance Murdock
S33. Captain McCallister
S34. Blinky the 3-Eyed Fish
S35. Ms. Botz
S36. Troy McClure
S37. Dr. Nick Riviera
S38. Barney Gumble
S39. McBain
S40. Character Checklist

Itchy & Scratchy Cards
I1. Bone Appetit
I2. Strike Three, You're Dead
I3. Pleased to Beat You
I4. Gentlemen Prefer Bombs
I5. Itchy & Scratchy On Ice
I6. Crocodile Doomdee
I7. A Farewell to Arms and Legs
I8. Tee-house of the August Kaboom
I9. Desperately Shrieking Scratchy
I10. Bongo Comics #1 cover
I11. Third Down, Dead to Go
I12. Gun with the Wind
I13. Little Dead Corvette
I14. Between-Meal Smacks
I15. Buzz Cola poster
I16. It's a Wonderful Knife
I17. Dead and Butter
I18. On the Road Again
I19. Some Like It Very, Very Hot
I20. The Dead Scratchy Society
I21. I'd Like To Propose a Toasting
I22. Flesh as a Daisy
I23. Out of the Frying Pan, Into the Grave
I24. Itchy Blandings Builds His Scream House
I25. Porch Pals
I26. Candlelight and Whine
I27. It Ain't the Heat, It's the Fatality
I28. Up, Up, and Oy Vay
I29. Itchy & Scratchy & Roger Meyers
I30. This Here Checklist

Radioactive Man Cards
R1. Fallout Boy
R2. Dr. Crab
R3. Radioactive Man
R4. Lava Man
R5. Radioactive Boy and Glowy
R6. 2 Loves of Radioactive Ape
R7. By My Sidekick Betrayed
R8. UnSecret Identity
R9. Public Enemy #1
R10. To Betroth A Foe

Wiggle Cards
W1. Maggie
W2. Itchy & Scratchy Anvil
W3. Containment Dome
W4. Itchy & Scratchy Chase
W5. Barney Belch
W6. Itchy & Scratchy Fan
W7. R-Man & Dr. Crab
W8. Homer Strangles Bart
W9. Bartman

Glow-In-The-Dark Cards
G1. Eyeballs
G2. Shock!
G3. Smilin' Joe
G4. TV

Cel Cards
C1. Base/Barber
C2. Middle/Barber
C3. Top/Barber
C4. Base/TV
C5. Middle/TV
C6. Top/TV

Tattoo Cards
1. Born to Chop
2. Burns Lizard

3. Flamethrower Itchy
4. Bart Fink
5. Mermaid Edna
6. Skull
7. Devil & Cat
8. Radioactive Man
9. Scratchy in Flames
10. Love/Hate

Promo Cards

B1. Homer On Couch
C1. Family Seated (Cel card to overlay B1)
P3. Bone Appetit
18. Otto The Busdriver

8 x 10 Promo card that contains the following:

P1. Otto The Busdriver
P2. Radioactive Man #27
P3. Bone Appetit
P4. Homer Simpson
(Given away with *Previews*, Vol.III, #10, October 1993.)

The Simpsons Trading Cards, Series II from Skybox. 1994. More of the same wonderful work seen in Series I. It's hard to imagine any fan not wanting these. What's really frightening is that *The Simpsons* actually had enough characters to justify a second series. Basic set (Character cards, Itchy & Scratchy cards, Bartman cards, Radioactive Man cards), $8-12. Wiggle cards, $1-3. Smell-O-Rama cards, $2-5 each. Disappearing Ink cards, $5-8 each. Arty Art cards, $30-40 each. Promo cards, $1-3 each, except for Bart Screen, $20-25 each.

The Disappearing Ink cards from the second Skybox Simpsons set: Bart Simpson, Principal Skinner, Itchy & Scratchy, Bartman.

The comics-only promo cards for the second Skybox set that appeared in selected Bongo comic titles. $1-3 each.

The Simpsons Trading Cards
Series II, SkyBox, 1994

Character Cards
S1. Principal Skinner
S2. Otto
S3. Lou & Eddie
S4. Human Fly
S5. Ned Flanders
S6. Laura Powers
S7. Montgomery Burns
S8. Smithers
S9. Marvin Monroe
S10. Bleeding Gums Murphy
S11. Dr. Hibbert
S12. Sherri & Terri
S13. Rev. Lovejoy
S14. Tattoo Guy
S15. Todd Flanders
S16. Santa's Little Helper
S17. The Devil
S18. Baby Bart
S19. Herman
S20. Hans Moleman
S21. Emily Winthrop
S22. Mr. Teeny
S23. Martin Prince
S24. Moe
S25. Mayor Quimby
S26. Leon Kompowski
S27. Snake
S28. Mrs. Bouvier
S29. Herb Powell
S30. Benjamin, Doug, & Gary
S31. Lionel Hutz
S32. Kearney
S33. Mindy Simmons
S34. Pepi
S35. Lunchlady Doris
S36. Ralph Wiggum
S37. Llewellyn Sinclair
S38. Kodos
S39. Jebediah Springfield
S40. Character Checklist

Itchy & Scratchy Cards
I1. Mow, Mow, Mow Your Throat
I2. Pop Goes the Scratchy
I3. This Spurting Life
I4. Fun Card / I Saw A Cat
I5. Down the Hatchet
I6. My Scratchy Dies Over the Ocean
I7. The Only Way to Fry
I8. Fun Card / Bombs Away
I9. Aorta be in Pictures
I10. Take Me Out to the Maul Game
I11. The Cat Who Slew Too Much
I12. Fun Card / Read Itchy's Mind
I13. The Blast Picture Show
I14. A Tomb with a Mew
I15. O Solo Meow
I16. Fun Card / Angel Scratchy
I17. That was Then, This is Pow!
I18. Field of Screams
I19. Fun Card / All the Cat's Horses
I20. You're Lookin' at It (Checklist)

Bartman Cards
B1. Houseboy
B2. Lisa the Conjuror
B3. Maggeena
B4. The Origin of Bart Dog
B5. The Angry Scotsman
B6. Camp Krusty's Krazy Daze
B7. The Penalizer
B8. Untold Tales of the Bart-signal
B9. Half-Nelson
B10. Checklist Card

Radioactive Man Cards
R1. Brain-O the Magnificent
R2. Bug Boy
R3. Plasmo the Mystic
R4. Larceny Lass.
R5. Black Partridge
R6. Bleeding Heart
R7. Hypno Head
R8. Captain Squid
R9. Weasel Woman
R10. The Containment Dome

Wiggle Cards
W1. Homer Donut
W2. Bartman Muscle
W3. I & S Knife
W4. Krusty
W5. Larva Kiss
W6. Chainsaw Scratchy
W7. Princess Kashmir
W8. I & S Strike
W9. Hypno Head

Arty Art Cards
(The Simpsons interpreted by other comic artists.)
A1. Mary Fleener
A2. Sam Kieth
A3. Gary Panter
A4. Jim Valentino

Smell-O-Rama Cards
1. Marge
2. Quimby
3. Homer
4. Snowball II
5. Maggie
6. Moe
7. Patty & Selma
8. Apu
9. Barney
10. Lunchlady Doris

Disappearing Ink Cards
D1. Principal Skinner
D2. Itchy & Scratchy
D3. Bartman
D4. Bart Simpson

Promo Cards
P2. Itchy & Scratchy In Stare-E-O
P3. Grampa Smell-O-Rama
B1. Willie "The Dupe" Dipkin (free with *Simpsons Comics* #4)
B2. Radioactive Man # 411 (free with *Radioactive Man* #4)
B3. Itchy & Scratchy Decoder Screen (free with *Itchy And Scratchy* #3)
(Used to decipher hidden messages on cards and in comics.)
B4. Black Belch Smell-O-Rama (free with *Simpsons Comics* #5)
B5. Bartman / Radioactive Man Spinner (free with *Bartman* #3)
B6. Radioactive Man, Atomic Avenger (free with *Radioactive Man* #5)
"Bart Screen" Decoder Card (available by mail order only)

The Simpsons Skycaps set. Skybox. Weeeeelllll, this might have been pushing it. An attempt to get in on the short lived pog fad, these bottlecap size *Simpsons* characters are fun, but nothing to get too excited about. Basic set, $6-10. Slammers, $1-3 each.

31. Skull of Death
32. Seymour Skinner
33. Otto Mann
34. Ned Flanders
35. Charles Montgomery Burns
36. Waylon Smithers
37. Dr. Marvin Monroe
38. Mr. Teeny
39. Todd Flanders
40. Santa's Little Helper
41. The Devil
42. Martin Prince
43. Moe
44. Mayor Quimby
45. Snake
46. Kearney
47. Pepi
48. Itchy The Mouse
49. Hypno Head
50. Barney Gumble

Hypno Slammers
1. Psych-O-Delic
2. Spiralina
3. Twirly-Gig
4. Tunnel Of Pain
5. The Mind Bender
6. Mr. Wobbly
7. Hypno-Mania
8. Throbbing Migraine
9. Swirl-O-Rama
10. Whirling Dervish

Simpsons SkyCaps (POGS).

Skybox, 1994

Skycaps
1. Homer J. Simpson
2. Marge Simpson
3. Bart Simpson
4. Lisa Simpson
5. Maggie Simpson
6. Clancy Wiggum
7. Kent Brockman
8. Sideshow Bob
9. Apu Nahasapeemapetilon
10. Edna Krabappel
11. Janey Powell
12. Nelson Muntz
13. Dr. Crab
14. Milhouse Van Houten
15. Captain Squid
16. Krusty The Clown
17. Groundskeeper Willie
18. Princess Kashmir
19. Larceny Lass
20. Patty & Selma Bouvier
21. Abraham "Grampa" Simpson
22. Smilin' Joe Fission
23. Weasel Woman
24. Troy McClure
25. Bleeding Heart
26. Lava Man
27. Fallout Boy
28. Ralph Wiggum
29. Bartman
30. Scratchy The Cat

The Simpsons Down Under card set from Tempo, 1996. This set from Australia leans heavily on the "Bart vs. Australia" episode, but includes the usual character cards and a bewildering array of clever chase cards. 15,000 boxes were produced. Basic set (Character cards, Bart vs. Australia cards, Tour of Springfield cards, and Checklists), $20-25. Homer As...cards, $4-8 each. Promo cards, $5-8. Springfield's Finest cards, $10-15 each. Seven Duffs cards, $10-15 each. Redemption cards, $20-30. Box cards, $40-50. Bartarang Exchange card, $75 and up.

The Simpsons Down Under
Collector Cards, Tempo, 1996

Character Cards
1. Homer J. Simpson
2. Marge Simpson
3. Abraham Grampa Simpson
4. Lisa Simpson
5. Bart Simpson
6. Maggie Simpson
7. Milhouse Van Houten
8. Uter
9. Ralph Wiggum
10. Waylon Smithers
11. Charles Montgomery Burns
12. Apu Nahasapeemapetilon
13. Sherri and Terri
14. Mr. Largo
15. Bag Boy
16. Snowball II
17. Santa's Little Helper
18. Itchy and Scratchy
19. Principal Skinner
20. Mrs. Krabappel
21. Groundskeeper Willie
22. Chief Wiggum
23. Lou and Eddie
24. Lionel Hutz
25. Moe
26. Barney Gumble
27. Snake
28. Ruth Powers
29. Princess Kashmir
30. Cletus and Brandine
31. Krusty the Clown
32. Sideshow Bob
33. Professor Frink
34. Kent Brockman
35. Troy McClure
36. Dr. Nick Riviera

Bart Vs Australia Cards
37. Header
38. Squeezing tubes
39. Lisa explaining to Bart
40. Bart Flushing Toilet
41. Homer in shower
42. Marge to Bart
43. Lisa at Globe with Bart
44. Bart spinning the Globe
45. Pointing to Australia
46. Koala being zapped
47. Bart and Tobias on the phone
48. Milhouse at window
49. Bart looking back at phone
50. Homer with the phone bill
51. Bruno Drondridge with the bill
52. Bruno on the phone with Bart
53. Bruno with his member of parliament
54. Prime Minister in the dam
55. Letters in Bart's bin
56. "No reason to block the TV"
57. Homer with the globe
58. On the couch with the guy
59. Arrival at Airport
60. Bart and his frog
61. Frog and Kangaroo
62. Homer and Marine, just as the punch lands
63. American guy at the toilet
64. Homer crying at toilet
65. Knifey Spoony
66. Giant beer
67. Bart apologising

68. The Aussie flag
69. Homer running to the boot
70. Boomerang throw
71. At the two kangaroos
72. Lisa with the Didgeridoo
73. Frogs in the shop
74. Running to the embassy
75. Bart with U.S. Flag behind him
76. Prime Minister at the gate
77. The boot through the gate
78. Don't tread on me
79. Cans being thrown at chopper
80. Frogs on the corn
81. Koala on the Helicopter leg

Zombie Puzzle Cards
82. Groundskeeper Willie and others
83. Dr. Hibbert and others
84. Grampa and others
85. Ned Flanders and others
86. Professor Frink and others
87. Apu and others
88. Homer and others
89. Lisa and others
90. Principal Skinner and others

Tour Of Springfield Cards
91. The Springfield Nuclear Power Plant
92. Jebediah Springfield Monument
93. Moe's Tavern
94. The Kwik-E-Mart
95. The Simpson Family Home
96. Springfield Elementary School

Checklist Cards
97. Tempo Card
98. Checklist 1
99. Checklist 2
100. Checklist 3

"Homer As..." Cards
HA1. An Indigenous Australian
HA2. Captain James Cook
HA3. Burke and Wills
HA4. Ned Kelly
HA5. Dame Edna Everage
HA6. Crocodile Dundee
HA7. Mad Max

Springfield's Finest Cards
SF1. Apu Nahasapeemapetilon
SF2. Montgomery Burns
SF3. Krusty The Clown
SF4. Nelson Muntz

The Seven Duffs
D1. Sleazy
D2. Tipsy
D3. Dizzy
D4. Edgy
D5. Surly
D6. Queasy
D7. Remorseful

Redemption Set
SDR1. Redemption Card
SDR2. America's Most Nuclear Family
SDR3. Certification Card

Box Cards
1. Party
2. Scream
3. Bart's Butt
4. Surfin' Dude

Bartarang Card
 B1. Bartarang Exchange Card

Promo Cards
 1-4. All 4 promo cards feature art from the cards in the basic set with advertising text.

The complete set of "Homer As..." cards from The Simpsons Down Under set. What, no Yahoo Serious?

Promo card that came with *Overstreet Comic Book Monthly*, Nov. 1993. $3-6.

Wallet cards from the U.K. $2-4 each.

Simpsons POG set from D.M.C. $8-12.

Unlicensed Bart sports cards. $6-10 set.

Top left:
Greeting cards from Gibson Greetings, 1991. $3-6 each.

Top right:
Greeting cards. Gibson, 1991. $3-6 each.

Bottom left:
Greetings cards. Gibson, 1994 and 1995. $3-6 each.

Bottom right:
Greetings cards. Gibson, 1995. $3-6 each.

Greeting cards. Gibson, 1995. $3-6 each.

Greeting cards. Gibson, 1995. $3-6 each.

Lisa greeting card, regular and die-cut version. Gibson, 1995. $3-6 each.

Greeting cards. Gibson, 1995. $3-6 each.

Greeting cards, embossed. Gibson, 1995. $3-6 each.

Chapter Ten: Promotional and Other

Promotional items, that is, items produced for the purposes of motivating station managers, store owners, and reviewers, are often the holy grails of collectors, partly because they're produced in such small quantities, but also because they tend to be more creative than the general run of collectibles. Consequently, these types of items are difficult, but not impossible, to find. However, their price can be somewhat prohibitive even if you are lucky enough to discover one.

Among the items produced for *The Simpsons* are tickets to *Itchy And Scratchy Land*; concert-style posters advertising the Homerpalooza and Spinal Tap episodes; a hockey puck emblazoned with Lisa to commemorate her short-lived career as a hockey player;

a laminated backstage pass for *Homerpalooza*; a *Duff Beer* mug that's marked *Property Of Moe's Tavern*, a gold record celebrating the success of The B-Sharps' *Baby On Board* and others that I'm sure have escaped my notice. Press kits, complete with publicity slides, surface from time to time.

A promotional item can also be something that wasn't produced for the general public, such as a store display, and we include a couple of examples here. Once again, these can be difficult to chase down but it doesn't hurt to ask the store manager what he plans to do with a display when he's finished. You might be pleasantly surprised.

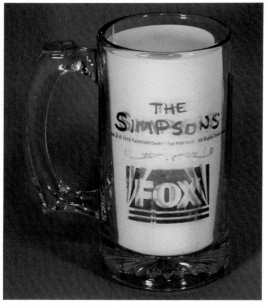

...you can find the Fox and Simpsons logos. $15-20.

Promo Duff Beer mug with Barney Gumble.
On the back...

Promo post card from Bongo. $3-5.
Promo Simpsons card from Skybox.
$3-5. Bongo Christmas card. $3-5.

Top left: Licensing and Merchandising sheet from Fox. $3-6.

Top center: Licensing and Merchandising sheet from Fox. $3-6.

Center left: Baby Bart steps out. Licensing and Merchandising sheet from Fox. $3-6.

Center: Licensing and Merchandising sheet from Fox, this one extolling the virtues of the forthcoming line of "Simpsons In The Dark" products. $3-6.

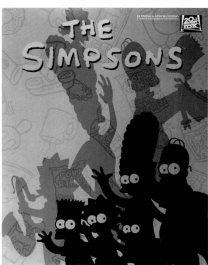

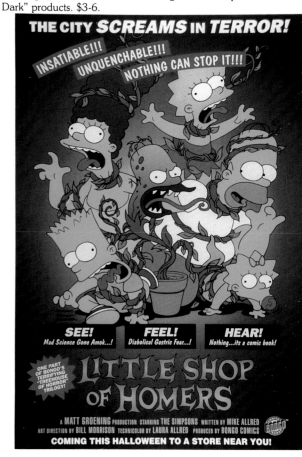

This promo poster for the "When Bongos Collide" comic crossover borrows the mural created by the free posters that came with Bongo's first four titles. $3-5.

Promo poster for "Little Shop Of Homers" from *Bart Simpson's Treehouse Of Horror #1*. $3-5.

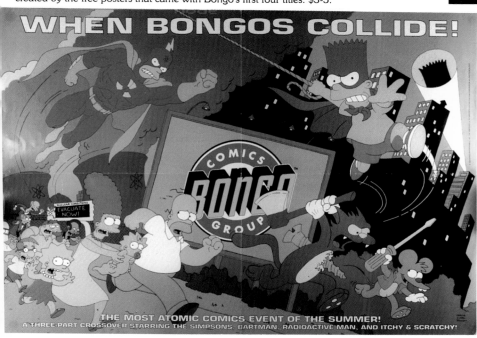

Top left: Promo poster for the "Who Shot Mr. Burns?" contest. $3-5.

Center left: Promo card from Vizir Detergent, Belgium. $5-8.

Top right: This CD divider was made available to stores to help promote the *Springfield* CD. Rhino. $5-8.

Bottom left: Homer and Lisa squirt rings from Kellogg's "Frosties" cereal, U.K. The complete set included Homer, Lisa, two Barts, Maggie, and Mr. Burns. $3-5 each.

Bottom right: *The Streets Of Springfield*, promo-only CD from Rhino. This disc features two medleys ("Theme Park" and "Overture") of tracks from the *Key Of Springfield* collection intended for radio play. $7-10.

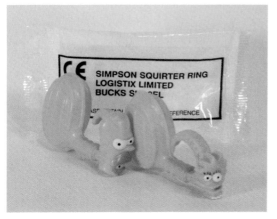

Above: Simpsons caps from the 100 cap set available in bags of Croky chips from Belgium. $2-4 each.

Center left: Promo version of *Songs In The Key Of Springfield* from Rhino Records. Some songs have their introductions placed into separate tracks for easier radio cueing. $15-20. Promo post card for *Springfield*. $3-5. Meanwhile...

Bottom left: ...on the backs, famed pitchman Troy McClure tries to put the rear ends in the seats.

Top right: Store display for *Songs In The Key Of Springfield*. Folds into CD tray. $7-10.

Bottom right: Album-size display cards for *Songs In The Key Of Springfield*. Turn them over...

Songs, score, and dialogue as heard on the hit TV show, including "Dr. Zaius," "We Do (The Stonecutters' Song)," "Flaming Moe's," the "Itchy & Scratchy" theme, along with variations of the "End Credits Theme." On CD and Cassette.

Who Shot Mr. Burns? T-shirt from Pepsi and 7-11. This shirt was available only through a mail-order offer. *Courtesy of Mike Nagle.* $8-12.

...and you'll find punch-out Bart and Homer heads. Liven up that spartan den. $7-10

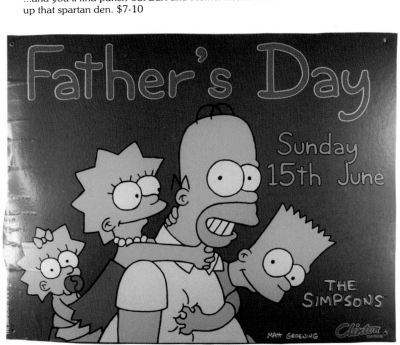

Songs In The Key Of Springfield T-shirt from Rhino Records. This shirt was given away for promotional purposes but was also available exclusively through the Rhino catalog. $15-20.

Father's Day sign from Clinton Cards, U.K. $7-10.

Display card from Subway's 1997 Simpsons toys promotion. The four toys were attached to this display with twist ties. $20-30.

Butterfinger Bart stand-up from Nestle. 3 ft. tall. $15-20.

6 ft. Homer Simpson stand-up. This promotional stand-up was created to help stores publicize the Simpsons House Give-Away in 1997. A Marge and Maggie stand-up was also made. Pepsi. $20-30.

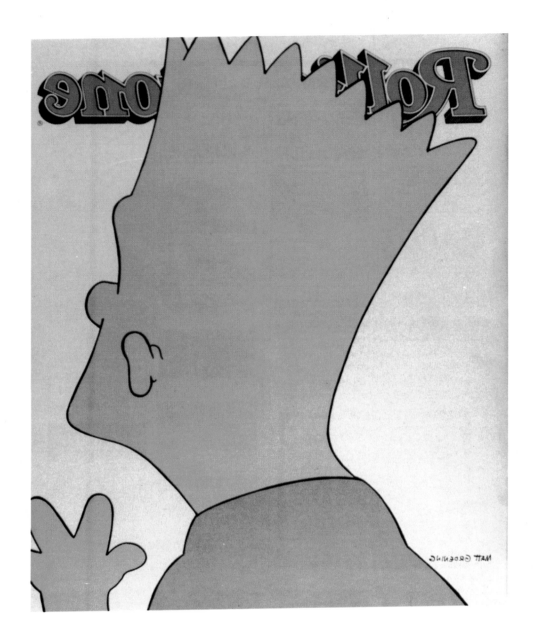

Bibliography

Carter, Gary. "CBM Interview with Matt Groening and Steve and Cindy Vance." *Overstreet Comic Book Monthly,* November 1993, #7: pp.10-16.

Getz, Robert W. "Home Sweet Homer: Collecting Simpsons Toys." *Toy Shop,* 18 July 1997, #373: pp.193.

Groening, Matt. *The Simpsons: A Complete Guide To Our Favorite Family.* HarperPerennial, 1997.

_____. "47 Secrets About The Simpsons, A Poem Of Sorts, And Some Filler." *Bartman,* # 4.

_____. "The Hitherto Untold Secret Origin Of A Certain Notorious Spiky-Haired Cartoon Character." *Simpsons Comics,* # 20.

Groth, Gary. "Matt Groening: An Interview." *The Comics Journal,* April 1991: pp. 78-95.

Holly, Rob. "The Simpsons' Father Speaks!" *Cards Illustrated,* September 1994, #9: pp. 30-33.

Martin, Warren, and Wood, Adrian. *I Can't Believe It's An Unofficial Simpsons Guide.* Virgin, 1997.

Tucker, Ken. "Bring It On, Homer!" *Entertainment Weekly,* 4 April 1997, #373: pp. 71-73.

Zehme, Bill. "The Only Real People On T.V." Rolling Stone, 28 June 1990, #581: pp. 41-47.